D1548640

Teaching Powerful Personal Narratives

STRATEGIES FOR COLLEGE APPLICATIONS AND HIGH SCHOOL CLASSROOMS

Teaching Powerful Personal Narratives

STRATEGIES FOR COLLEGE APPLICATIONS AND HIGH SCHOOL CLASSROOMS

Mary Jane Reed

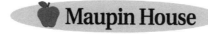

MAUPIN HOUSE PUBLISHING

Teaching Powerful Personal Narratives:
Strategies for College Applications and High School Classrooms

by **Mary Jane Reed**

© 2004 Mary Jane Reed. All Rights Reserved

Cover, Compact Disc, and Book Design | Hank McAfee

Editor | Mark Devish

Library of Congress Cataloging-in-Publication Data

Reed, Mary Jane, 1940-
Teaching powerful personal narratives : strategies for college applications and high school classrooms / Mary Jane Reed.
   p. cm.
  ISBN 0-929895-78-9 (pbk. with CD)
  1. College applications--United States. 2. Exposition (Rhetoric) 3. Academic writing. I. Title.
  LB2353.2.R44 2004
  378.1'616--dc22
                    2004024251

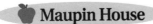

Maupin House Publishing, Inc.
PO Box 90148
Gainesville, FL 32607
1-800-524-0634 / 352-373-5588
352-373-5546 (fax)
www.maupinhouse.com
info@maupinhouse.com

Publishing Professional Resources that Improve Classroom Performance

The author and publisher are grateful to the following universities for
their cooperation in allowing their college essay questions to be reproduced:

Georgetown University

Massachusetts Institute of Technology

Southern Methodist University

George Washington University

University of Notre Dame

Northwestern University

Princeton University

University of Pennsylvania

The University of North Carolina at Chapel Hill

University of Virginia

Marquette University

Ohio Wesleyan University

Wake Forest University

University of Michigan

The Ohio State University

Some examples of student work have been edited for space and content.

For Jamie and Kristen
my rainbow and roses

CONTENTS

My appreciation to

Anne Johns   Solon High School College Counselor

Alice Morgan   Guidance Department Chair, and all the members of the Guidance Department for their help and gracious hospitality when I return each fall

Joseph V. Regano   Superintendent of Solon City Schools, who helped make it all happen

All the students who diligently traveled that lonely road of revision—and especially those whose essays are included in this book. It was my pleasure to have worked with each and every one of them.

INTRODUCTION

The personal narrative may be the most important genre for high school students to master. It is, after all, the genre of the college application essay—arguably the first life-altering writing assignment that students will encounter in their young lives. But the personal narrative is also the genre that often gives students their first opportunity at a different life-altering discovery: the writing voices they will work with the rest of their academic and professional careers. Personal narratives can foster creative explorations which build confidence in students' written communication.

Originally, I wanted to write a book that was focused solely on helping high school teachers help their students write essays that would get them into college. Every year, juniors and seniors bombard their English teachers with requests for advice on writing successful college application essays, and often teachers don't know how to offer the most effective assistance. The shelves of bookstores and libraries are full of manuals that offer advice to students on how to write successful college essays, but I could not find any books that compiled information useful to high school teachers: how essays are factored into the application process, who reads them, how they are assessed, what universities perceive as good essays, what topics students should avoid, how to modify essays to comply with length restrictions, and how students should approach each question in the application to provide a comprehensive profile of themselves. I believe knowing this information is extremely important and will allow you to offer informed advice that will help your students write better application essays.

However, the college application essay should be the culmination of students' exposure to the personal narrative, not their introduction. Perhaps due to the emphasis placed on teaching literature and the need for meeting the criteria required of state-assessment exams, traditional high school language-arts programs generally put more focus on the analysis of fiction. As a result, the thrust of the writing done in many curriculums ends up being analytical: the use of persona in Gulliver's adventures, Milkman's search to discover his roots, Golding's use of symbolism. And while analytical writing certainly is a crucial part of any well-developed language arts curriculum, narrative writing is sorely missed when it is only touched upon or is neglected altogether.

As I worked on this book, I realized that much of the information that would help teachers help their students write better college-application essays would also allow teachers to teach their students the basics of the personal narrative. I can't encourage teachers strongly enough to include more narrative-writing in their curriculums. Students should be exposed to the personal narrative no matter what grade they are in.

I've designed this book to be useful. It doesn't matter if you currently teach a complete narrative-writing unit as part of your regular curriculum or if you just want to introduce an occasional narrative assignment into your schedule: you'll find something here that you can use. The components of good narrative writing have been divided into different chapters (discovering a topic, voice, the importance of details, revision) that you can use "a la carte" to help your students with the skills that they need to focus on. The handouts and supplements will be valuable for any teacher who teaches any amount of narrative to their high school students.

The information presented here is a vitamin shot, a supplement to promote the health of narrative writing in your classroom. While much of the information is tailored specifically for teachers with students who are working on college-application essays, all of it can be customized to help any student with any narrative writing. §

CHAPTER 1

From Assignments to Admissions

When working on personal narratives, writers must chart their own courses down lonely roads, independently exploring, probing, and prodding themselves for information and inspiration. It is easy for students to become overwhelmed by the solitude of the experience: there are no texts to use for research, no thesis-driven format to help shape their compositions. And when the pressure of writing a personal essay is combined with the do-or-die necessity of applying for colleges, the task becomes especially daunting. To be successful, these hopeful seniors obviously must rely on the writing skills they have acquired in their English classes. Unfortunately, many high school English teachers currently don't devote much time to teaching narratives—some don't include them at all—undoubtedly because their curriculums are already laden with the analysis of literature.

Writing personal narratives (whether for a college application or as an English class assignment) is a valuable experience. They provide outlets for students to indulge their creativity, develop their style, and cultivate their writing voices. Personal narratives are about them, their experiences, reactions, and observations. They reflect students' ability to probe, to question, and even confront the unanswerable questions that life often poses. Writing a personal narrative provides students with ample freedom to take charge of their writing, to think of themselves as "writers" unencumbered (within the parameters of the assignment) by "what the teacher wants." Within these essays their individuality surfaces as they demonstrate their passion, convictions, and reactions. A successful personal narrative reflects the many decisions writers must make involving inclusions, omissions, revisions, and the angst that plagues all writers seeking acceptance.

Needless to say the college application essay is one narrative that most students pursue vigorously. Because students realize the importance of this particular essay—and correctly perceive it as an investment in their future—they often regard it as the most pragmatic exercise in the language arts curriculum. Searching for perfection, they are receptive to suggestions and actively engage in executing numerous drafts. While those applying to competitive colleges are eager to begin the process at the beginning of the school year because of early decision and the prospect of having to write numerous essays for each college, others may dawdle the first semester away and take their chances with rolling admissions. Regardless, all seniors are united by one universal purpose—acceptance into the college of their choice.

Their bounty is receiving that nervously anticipated "fat" envelope inviting them to become part of the incoming freshman class. And this is no small task these days when many of the popular selective schools are flooded with applications from students who reflect outstanding academic performance throughout high school. They have impressive SAT/ACT scores, good GPA's in rigorous courses of study, strong recommendations, and a myriad of activities: serving as presidents of their class, being captains of football and soccer teams, volunteering for hours of community service, etc. So what gives those accepted by prestigious schools the cutting edge? Something that sets them apart. Bill Paul cites in his book *Getting In: Inside the College Admissions Process* some of the caliber of activities that successful Princeton candidates brought to their applications: inventing a talking measuring cup for the blind, establishing the first high school chapter of Habitat for Humanity, publishing a children's book, etc. (24).

The competition is fierce. Even state schools are becoming more competitive with the spiraling cost of tuition, room and board and expenses at many private schools reaching around $40,000 per year. With this kind of pressure confronting seniors—and their parents—the college essay becomes more and more important each year, for it portrays the applicant in a way that all the statistics in the application cannot.

Who Reads Personal Narratives?

Experienced authors always consider their audience before beginning, and as English teachers we know all too well that writing an article for *The New York Times* is vastly different than writing a proposal for a state grant. Whether your students are working on essays that only you will see or are crafting responses for their college applications, encourage them to keep their audience in mind.

The reader of the college essay is a member of the admissions committee who will be reading thousands of essays. At some universities the committee consists exclusively of admissions officers, at others it can include staff as well. At Cornell University, for example, faculty members are actively involved in the decision process. According to Kay Wagner, chair of a regional committee that reads essays, the faculty looks for students who will be "intellectually engaged in the classroom, students who grapple with material and are not concerned exclusively with what's on the exam" (Telephone

Interview 24 September 2003). Most universities and colleges give each essay two readings. At some schools regional representatives provide the second reading of those essays written by students in the schools within their region.

Writing an essay for a college admissions committee can be one of the most intimidating tasks for students because of the high stakes involved. Students often strive to make a big splash in the sea of essays confronting the selection committee. Though students must contend with how they will be perceived, they must embrace the tenets of good writing—to express genuine feelings candidly, clearly, and concisely while maintaining a distinct voice throughout. In speaking with admissions officers throughout the country, I have found that they are basically offering the same advice to students: Don't write to impress. Just be yourself. But for these young writers, the temptation to over inflate their language and their personalities is always there. Encourage your students to ignore it.

Scott Schamberger, admissions counselor at Emory University reinforced this message. "Essays should help us get to know the student better. They are good support for what is seen elsewhere in the application." When asked what some of the apparent weaknesses he has observed in reading essays, he responded, "students trying to be someone they are not. They try to impress with SAT words. We know the type of language 17-year-olds use." He also cautioned students in attempting to develop an essay focusing on "life-altering" experiences. "Some of the best essays describe every day occurrences as something unique, special." (Telephone interview, 19 September 2003).

Teachers, too, know the frustration of reading personal narratives filled with overblown language and overstated beliefs. Remind your students to keep their language simple and their focus clear. Let them know that you'll be more impressed with writing that relays information clearly than with writing that strives too hard to be clever.

Personal Involvement, Personal Beliefs

My interest in the personal narrative evolved after twenty-five years of teaching senior English and serving on various curriculum committees. During that time, I thought I knew how to prepare my students for their college application essays. But—while I wasn't necessarily giving my students bad advice—it wasn't until my school board lured me out of retirement and hired me as a writing consultant to help launch a unique college program that I researched some key information that allowed me to help students beyond their misplaced modifiers and general wordiness: how essays are factored into the application process, who reads them, how they are assessed, what universities perceive as good essays, what topics students should avoid, how to modify essays to comply with length restrictions, and how students should approach each question in the application to provide a comprehensive profile of themselves. Knowing this information is extremely important and will allow any high school teacher to offer informed advice that will help students write better personal narratives in general and application essays in specific.

As an adjunct to the guidance department each fall, I meet with seniors in twenty-minute conferences and guide them through the process of writing their application essays. When the program was first piloted, I naively wondered if I would spend much of my day twiddling away time in seclusion, waiting for a single student to appear. I was haunted by recurring questions: Would any of the 400 seniors sign up for these voluntary conferences? Would they be receptive to the information and advice I'd be able to give them?

My fears proved to be unfounded. After word-of-mouth recommendations were passed along by the first participants, I was overrun with responses. The students—although certainly not neglected by their regular teachers—seemed to crave the hands-on audience I offered. They couldn't believe that a teacher would be on duty all day just to help them with their college essays. I conducted over 800 individual conferences those first three months of school. Although the sign-up sheet stated that conferences would begin at 7:30 a.m. and end at 3:30 p.m., students began redesigning the schedule, penciling in 7 a.m. starts and adding appointments that began long after school was over. Because I knew many seniors had study halls during lunchtime and therefore would be free to attend a session, I scheduled no lunches for myself. It's amazing how long a sandwich can last when it is consumed in small bites throughout the afternoon.

After repeatedly modeling the two biggest strengths of good narrative writing—the all-important angle and an engaging voice sustained by ample descriptions and details—I found I was establishing a consistent, sequential process for the development of successful narratives. Students recognized that our approach together made sense and provided progress at every step. Because of the intense individualization (and piecemeal revisions), many became better writers in those three brief months. One student, at the end of our time together, surveyed the many drafts of his college essay. "This wasn't just an assignment," he said. "This was a course in writing!"

Indeed it was. Parents, too, witnessed the progress and success that their child experienced. And nothing insures the longevity of a program like parental support. To get the parents involved in the application process the Guidance Department sponsored a "college night." Hundreds of invitations were sent to junior and senior parents. My participation involved explaining to parents my approach in helping their children address the college essay and in "packaging" themselves throughout an entire application. I assured them that my part was to support and implement the work of the English Department. After all, the college essay does not just happen the senior year. It is a result of a solid and sequential writing program where English teachers work with students each year on developing their writing skills. By the time our students were seniors, they basically could write. What they needed in this final year was intense work on revising content and refining their use of language in addition to learning the savvy of completing applications that would reflect their diverse backgrounds and experiences. My faith in the writing program was confirmed when students began receiving hand-written notes and e-mails from admissions officers stating how much they enjoyed reading their essays.

I believe that developing a personal narrative can teach a writer the craft of writing more efficiently than other genres of writing. That's why I think it's so important to include narratives in your curriculum. To help you do that, I've included materials that will allow you to easily feature the genre in your classroom: a CD of handouts that you can customize and reproduce for your students, transparency masters that you can produce and use during discussions, and samples of student essays that demonstrate the importance of voice. For those of you with students getting ready to apply for college, I've included strategies for starting—and revising—application essays, chapters on the types of application questions your students may be asked to address, and models of conferencing, both individual and "collective conferencing." I've also included a chapter on writing college recommendations, as you will surely be asked to pen a few.

A Note on Conferencing

Ideally, teaching the personal narrative as part of the high school English curriculum would entail classroom teachers introducing the assignments, giving students time to independently work on them, and then meeting with the students in periodic one-on-one conferences as the drafts evolve. But realistically, you and I know that teachers simply do not have the time to conduct multiple conferences with each individual student. Teachers are already pressed to complete their given curriculums as they tend to various state demands of proficiency—all while teaching five or more classes. However, some form of conferencing can readily improve your students' progress as they learn to work with the personal narrative.

Individual conferencing can be time consuming, but it can also be extremely beneficial. The confidentiality of an individual conference is comforting, and students appreciate the personalized attention. Even offering five minutes one-on-one before or after school can be very meaningful—especially for those working on a sensitive topic or those who are not confident writers. Chapter Three provides suggestions for conducting individual conferences and models three examples of initial individual conferences that helped students discover a workable topic.

If funding for education were not a problem in this country today, a more individualized approach to teaching writing could emerge. Some schools already host in-house writing centers where English teachers are on duty every period of the day to help walk-ins individually with their writing problems. If your school offers such a program, you should encourage your students to take advantage of it.

Small group conferencing is another effective option. Organizing a class into small groups that share common issues can save you time and allow students the opportunity to exchange ideas among themselves. After assessing a set of essays, categorize them into piles that share common topics or similar problems such as lack of details and specific examples, a weak beginning, undeveloped ideas, areas that rely on telling instead of showing, etc. The next day—after reviewing the criteria for the assignment with the class—return the papers and assign students into groups where they can keep exchanging papers until everyone in the group has read the others' essays. Tell them to discuss their reactions to their partners' essays. (Depending on the length of your class period, the group discussion may have to take place the next day.) Encourage them to specifically cite what they think are each essay's strengths and weaknesses.

As your students talk, stroll from group to group, monitoring the discussions and taking mental notes that will help you address student concerns. Briefly meet with each group. The process helps students to become more confident with their writing skills, for they realize that others, too, share common problems and struggle with expressing themselves successfully—that writing is difficult for everyone. And those stellar passages that produce "wow" reactions from their peers demonstrate how effective writing can be when it works.

The "**collective conference**" (discussed in Chapter Seven) is an approach I created while teaching because of my frustration with not being able to help students individually when I returned their essays. The transparencies created while grading essays would highlight in class portions of successful essays in addition to the concerns that needed revision. This approach helped me to address student needs within a single class period. Often before essays were returned near the end of class, students would sheepishly admit that they knew what they did wrong, and some even correctly anticipated their grades.

Use whatever method of conferencing will fit into your schedule. Remember, the goal is to get your students to experience writing personal narratives before they sit down to work on their college application essays. Not only will they present stronger applications, they will become better writers. §

CHAPTER 2

Types of Personal Narrative Questions

As you expose your students to the genre of the personal narrative, you should have them work with different types of narrative questions. Using the questions that colleges and universities ask on their applications is a good way to expose them to real world examples. Plus, being familiar with the different types of questions your students are going to be asked to respond to will help you understand the ways that you can help them prepare for their application essays.

College application questions range from general "tell us about you" questions to very specific and creative ones. Some students will write only one application essay while others will be inundated with many. The random examples cited below represent some of the questions colleges and universities have posed.

"You" Questions

- The Admissions Committee would like to know more about you in your own words. Please submit a brief essay, either autobiographical or creative, which you feel best describes you.

  Georgetown University

- The Admission Committee would like to know some of the things that you are thinking, laughing, or talking about at this time in your life.

  Southern Methodist University

- Compose a Personal Statement with content of your own choosing. In doing so, feel free to introduce yourself to us in any way you feel appropriate. Whether your essay is autobiographical or imaginative, it should reflect who you are in both form and content.

  University of Notre Dame

- Since we are interested in who you are as well as what you can do, please briefly tell us about yourself. Please feel free to describe an experience to help you clarify your point.

  Princeton University

- How is the person you know yourself to be different from the person your family and friends know you to be?

  The University of North Carolina at Chapel Hill

- An application to MIT is much more than a set of test scores, grades and activities. It's often a reflection of an applicant's dreams and aspirations, dreams shaped by the worlds we inhabit. We'd like to know a bit more about your world. Describe the world you come from, for example your family, clubs, school, community, city, or town. How has that world shaped your dreams and aspirations?

- Life brings many disappointments as well as satisfactions. Could you tell us about a time in your life when you experienced disappointment, or faced difficult or trying circumstances? How did you react?

  Massachusetts Institute of Technology

Upbeat, Creative Questions

- If you were president of the United States for a day, what one policy—whether serious or semi-serious—would you implement? Why?

- The memoir has become an increasingly popular genre among American writers. For example, Carolina's own Charles Kuralt named his *Life on the Road*; Mia Hamm called hers *Go for the Goal: A Champion's Guide to Winning in Soccer and Life*. If you were to write a memoir that covered your life from birth through high school, what would you choose for your title? Why?

  The University of North Carolina at Chapel Hill

- Design your own monument. (Case in point: The Vietnam Veterans Memorial was designed by college student Maya Lin Ying, who at age 21 was commissioned to design the memorial after competing nationally for the honor.) Now it is your turn to immortalize a moment, an event, a person, a generation, an icon. Describe what your national monument would commemorate or celebrate. (This question is meant to both stimulate your creativity and allow you to distinguish yourself from other applicants!)

  George Washington University

- In his autobiography *Long Walk to Freedom*, Nelson Mandela reflects upon his life and commitment to the anti-apartheid movement. He writes: "I learned that courage was not the absence of fear, but the triumph over it." Give a personal example of how courage has played a role in your life.

- English poet W.H. Auden wrote, "Those who will not reason perish in the act; those who will not act perish for that reason." At Notre Dame, we value equally intellectual inquiry and social responsibility. Describe a personal experience in which your ideas motivated your actions, or an experience in which your actions changed your ideas.

  University of Notre Dame

- We can be defined not only by what we choose to keep but what we choose to discard. Write about something you reluctantly chose to discard and why this was a difficult choice.

- Emily Dickinson wrote, "The Possible's slow fuse is lit/By the Imagination." When has imagination sparked a change in what you considered possible? How did this experience affect you?

- A number of significant people were practically unknown to the general public in their lifetimes: Franz Kafka, Rosalind Franklin, Vincent van Gogh. Select a living person whose work or message is overlooked, and explain why you feel this person will achieve importance in the future.

  Northwestern University

- You have just completed your 300-page autobiography. Please submit page 217.

  University of Pennsylvania

- What is your favorite word, and why?

- Look out any window in your home. What would you change about what you see?

  University of Virginia

- You are about to embark on a lengthy road trip in a two-passenger car with no radio. What person—real or fictional—would you choose to accompany you and why?

  Marquette University

- If you could invent one thing, what would you invent? Why? How would humanity benefit from this invention? What would be the negative effects, if any, of your invention?

  Ohio Wesleyan University

- For what cause would you lead a march on Washington, D.C.?

  Wake Forest University

Questions on Diversity

Questions regarding diversity are springing up in college applications, no doubt a result of the Supreme Court's June 23, 2003 affirmative action ruling regarding the University of Michigan's point-based admissions system. (Points—assigned to factors such as GPA, types of classes taken, and athletics, etc.—are used by many schools to rank students' applications.) The ruling allows universities to consider race as a part of the application process, but they cannot—as they used to—assign points to students for being minorities. As a result, many universities are assessing students holistically and have begun to ask students to respond to questions concerning diversity. For instance, for the first time, The Ohio State University required applicants seeking admission for the fall of 2004 to address four essay questions, one of which pertains to diversity. According to Beth Heiser, associate director of undergraduate admissions, this method of review complies with the Supreme Court ruling. Plus, the four short essays will provide more information from the students, presenting a more complete picture of their high school background. "We feel this is the best way to get information" (Telephone interview, 8 October 2003).

The university redesigned its essay format for students seeking admission for the fall of 2005. It now requires students to answer two essay questions in 200 words each. Every student has to answer the first question:

- The character of the Ohio State community is a reflection of the diverse interests, talents, backgrounds, experiences, strengths, and perspectives of its students, faculty, and staff. What do you believe you will contribute to this university community?

Next, students are asked to address one of these two questions:

- Imagine you have the opportunity to have a conversation with and ask questions of a person from history. Who would that person be, what would you ask, and why?

- Advancements in technology may benefit humanity or may come at the risk of doing harm. Identify a technological advancement that you regard as an example of this dilemma and discuss your thoughts about future implications.

As assignments in a high school English class, questions about diversity can serve as fodder for discussion and as exercises in self-discovery.

Questions on the Common Application

The Common Application is popular with students because it simplifies the process of applying to multiple schools. Over 250 colleges and universities use the Common Application, some exclusively (meaning they have no institution-specific form at all). If students are applying to many colleges, they may only have to complete one application—and they can submit it electronically if they wish to do so. (See www.commonapp.org for a list of participating institutions.)

These are the directions and "you" type essay questions included in the Common Application:

> "This personal statement helps us become acquainted with you in ways different from courses, grades, test scores, and other objective data. It will demonstrate your ability to organize thoughts and express yourself. We are looking for an essay that will help us know you better as a person and as a student. Please write an essay (250-500 words) on a topic of your choice or on one of the options listed below…"

1. Evaluate a significant experience, achievement, risk you have taken, or ethical dilemma you have faced and its impact on you.

2. Discuss some issue of personal, local, national, or international concern and its importance to you.

3. Indicate a person who has had a significant influence on you, and describe that influence.

4. Describe a character in fiction, an historical figure, or a creative work (as in art, music, science, etc.) that has had an influence on you, and explain that influence.

5. A range of academic interests, personal perspectives, and life experiences adds much to the educational mix. Given your personal background, describe an experience that illustrates what you would bring to the diversity in a college community, or an encounter that demonstrated the importance of diversity to you.

6. Topic of your choice.

A word of caution: It is important for students to review the instructions of each individual university to which they are applying. Schools that accept the Common Application may also request additional information such as a supplemental essay or a graded one from an English class. Some schools have special instructions pertaining to Early Decision. Also, admissions officers advise students who use the Common Application to be sure they address the appropriate university with each application. It's all too easy to send an application addressing Denison University to DePauw University. And students should be sure to spell and cite the name of the university correctly. The University of Notre Dame, for instance, is not Notre Dame University.

The Composite of Application Questions in a Single Application

Being comfortable with different types of essay questions is a major advantage for students since they can present a composite of themselves by carefully (and confidently) choosing which college application essays to answer. Colleges and universities use a certain psychology when designing their essay questions. Since relatively dry information (grade point average, class rank, standardized test scores, and extracurricular activities) comprises the basic data of a student's application, schools need the essay questions to provide three-dimensional insight into the student's character, special talents, and personality. Encourage your students to determine how to provide the most diverse profile possible by examining all the required and optional questions in a single application and developing a plan to highlight their interests before beginning to address any one of them.

The application designed by the University of Michigan for its 2005 incoming freshmen illustrates how a composite of essay questions can probe a broad spectrum of a senior's life beyond the statistics. For example, all applicants have to answer this question in about 250 words.

- At the University of Michigan we are committed to building a superb educational community with students of diverse talents, experiences, opinions, and cultural backgrounds. What would you as an individual bring to our campus community?

This question focuses on diversity and is in accordance with the Supreme Court's 2003 ruling. It reflects the university's continuing commitment to building a culturally diverse community of academically talented students. In working with students I have found this question provides them with an opportunity to discuss the circumstances of their ethnic and/or racial backgrounds as well as the talents and achievements that set them apart from other students.

The second 250-word essay question involves nine options where students address the question that pertains to the school or college to which they are applying. For example, freshmen and dual degree applicants applying to the College of Literature, Science, and the Arts must respond to the following question:

- What led you to choose area(s) of academic interest that you have listed in your application to the University of Michigan? If you are undecided, what areas are you most interested in, and why?

This question opens an avenue for students to describe a meaningful experience that motivates them to pursue a particular field of study. For example, a student may have been involved in an internship or mentoring program that provided him/her the opportunity to shadow professionals who work at hospitals, law firms, social service agencies, etc.

For students applying to the School of Music, a modern day dilemma confronts them in this question:

- Imagine you have been asked to present a statement to your local School Board in favor of retaining the high school's performing arts programs, all threatened by budget cuts. What would you tell them?

Now here's an opportunity to defend the performances of Handel's *Messiah*, Prokofiev's *Romeo and Juliet* ballet, *West Side Story*, each representing options that uplift the soul of individuals who learn to appreciate music and the arts lest we become like Gulliver's illiberal Houyhnhnms.

Another interesting question challenges those applying to the School of Art & Design:

- Compare and contrast an actual apple, a two-dimensional image of an apple, and a three-dimensional replica of an apple.

I imagine few English teachers could offer any input on addressing this one even though imagery is the heart of poetry. But I would enjoy reading an essay that could teach me how to view an apple in multiple images.

After the 250-word essays are addressed, all applicants must address one of these questions in approximately 500 words:

- Describe a setback or ethical dilemma that you have faced. How did you resolve it? How did the outcome affect you? If something similar happened in the future, how would you react?

- Discuss an issue of local, national, or international concern. Why is this issue important to you? How do you think it should be addressed?

- Some writers suggest that by tradition science is concerned with truth while art is concerned with beauty. How might these two endeavors be the same? How might they be irreconcilably different?

These questions are comprehensive and require an introspective search. Asking teens to discuss how a failure or an ethical dilemma affected them (and then to evaluate their actions) is a tall order especially if they are having trouble letting go of the notion that they can only write essays that reveal the rosier sides of their existence. Answering this first question, then, requires a candid, rational, insightful approach.

To address the second question successfully students need to be well-read and attuned to a world far beyond football games and rock concerts. Students found that selecting an issue was reasonable but offering a resolution and showing how it would affect others was challenging. They had to be on guard not to appear simplistic in their approach and wallow in generalities.

The third question seeks an intellectual and creative response to the age-old quest to contrast and reconcile truth with beauty. It's steeped in the liberal arts, requiring students to merge their experience with science and an appreciation of the arts.

Regardless of which questions your students answer, this composite of options provides them with an expansive outlet to introduce themselves to the admissions readers in a broad profile that highlights their personality, intellectual verve, concerns, strengths, creativity, writing skills, and potential to succeed in a college environment. By carefully answering these questions, students are addressing what readers want to discover in the underlying directive: "Tell us about yourself."

Helpful Suggestions for Common Issues

- Some universities offer a "last-chance" essay at the end of the application inviting students to include another essay if there's still something they would like to share not included in the application. Even if a question is optional, students should be encouraged to answer it. Taking advantage of every opportunity to share an additional interest or activity helps to develop a more comprehensive profile of that student.

- A word about length. Usually, colleges will specify the length for the essay (often 250-500 words). These are guidelines for students to consider, but unfortunately for some, the restriction on length can be an inhibiting factor that blocks the development of ideas. Students become so intent in adhering to the specified number of words that they are reluctant to provide examples and details that are so vital to good writing. In brainstorming and banging out the first draft, students should cast aside the length restriction and provide more specific examples and details than are needed. Reducing and condensing are easier during the revision stages than trying to develop ideas to build a quality essay.

- Students should bring two copies of a draft when seeking help—one for you as their writing coach, and one for them to mark the areas that need to be reworked and revised based on your suggestions. This helps students to maintain control as writers while helping you to make suggestions without becoming invasive. Also, you should encourage students who are seeking help to include verbatim the question they are responding to at the top of their essays. Sometimes you can correct or reinterpret a student's understanding of the question.

- Of all the writing assignments seniors complete, the college application essay readily draws the attention of parents who eagerly review the evolving drafts. Indeed, they have a vested interest in the application process since they will be paying the tuition bills. And I'm sure they can provide meaningful input. But so often they lobby to attach a concluding paragraph at the end of a creative narrative that tells directly how conscientious and talented their child is. They do not realize that showing through a descriptive scenario communicates more than the writer's character and talents. It illustrates creativity and the ability to organize and express ideas clearly and concisely, to develop a commanding voice that makes the reader think and appreciate the quality of writing. Injecting or attaching directives only detracts from the essence of the work. Perhaps communicating with parents in PTA meetings, on websites, or during curriculum night (open house) can help to assure them that the staff is committed to helping their child create a well-written essay. §

CHAPTER 3

Beginning the Process

Whether your students are about to undertake their college application essays or are getting ready to write an essay for your English class, it is a good idea to remind them about the task they are about to perform. **Handout #1** (on the included CD) gives an overview of some of the more important points they need to remember. I suggest you distribute it the first time you discuss personal narratives, and then remind your students of its contents from time to time. I think it's especially important to revisit it with those students who are about to begin their college applications, even if they've already seen it. All the seniors at my school receive a copy during the senior class meeting the first week of school.

▶ HANDOUT #1 ◀

Writing Personal Narratives

A personal narrative is a reflection of you. It can reveal your personality, interests, concerns, reactions, observations, and even your sense of humor. It's your story, and it should say more about you than any other writing you may ever do.

- If you are having trouble selecting a topic, begin by jotting down a list of events and interests that you have pursued such as activities and hobbies that are meaningful to you, jobs, cultural and family events, unusual experiences, achievements, etc. Be creative while you brainstorm: You may have topics that would work well for the college essay and yet not fully realize it.

- After choosing your topic, brainstorm by jotting down an abundance of facts, incidents, reactions, etc. concerning your subject. You may not use many of the items listed, but collectively they can help you to narrow your search for the **focus** of the essay.

- Once the focus is established, develop it fully. This is your **angle**, your spin on the topic. It will rescue you from being trapped in chronological telling. For example, if you were a camp counselor, **describe** one day on the job or an incident with a child that would show how caring and patient you are and how you assume responsibility. If your subject is volunteering in a nursing home, focus on one patient or one incident and show how you reacted and what you learned.

- Let your readers draw conclusions. Do not **tell** them what you want them to know. **Show** them. They will know you are conscientious by reading how you resolve problems, how you confront conflict, or how you care for others. They will know you are talented by your description of the dance recital or the way you designed the computer program. They will enjoy your account of how you counseled reluctant eight-year-olds at soccer camp. They will know your perseverance in working at a fast-food take-out window.

- As you write, periodically ask yourself:

  How will I be perceived?

  Why would the reader *want* to continue reading my essay?

  Will it be remembered after it has been read?

- You do not have to fly around the world in an air balloon to develop an interesting essay. Your topic can be a very common one. **How** you reveal it will determine its quality. Remember, though it's tempting, **do not write to impress. Do not write what you think your reader wants to read**. Let your essay reflect thoughtfulness throughout. Whether it's a college admissions officer, your teacher, or a friend, your readers will be able to tell when you are writing from your heart.

- When writing your first draft, do not feel restricted by length limits that may be imposed on the assignment. College applications often require that essays fall between 250 and 500 words. Teachers sometimes will say that an essay can't be over three pages in length. Don't worry about exceeding these limits. Just bang the first draft out. It's easier to eliminate portions of the essay in the evolving drafts than it is to struggle for ideas later.

- Have courage. There will be many drafts. But I assure you, you will be proud of the essay you submit.

Finding a Topic

When students write the college essay (or any personal narrative), they should consider at the beginning how they will generate interest and engage their reader. This is no small task, for good narrative writing must lure the reader to continue turning pages even though TV, or video games, or the Internet awaits. (Even yard work may present a more interesting option if the narrative is tedious enough.) It's the "story" that's remembered long after an essay is read. After I share with students samples of topics that rendered successful essays in the past—the hassle of learning to drive a stick-shift Beetle that resisted going into reverse, the tribulations of being the mayor's daughter, the search for identity in the clash of two cultures—they begin to realize they do not have to create outlandish topics or "cutesy" approaches to impress the reader. The quality of writing enhances the piece because it is a genuine expression of feeling. Good writers don't have to travel into the wild like adventure writer Jon Krakauer or be involved in an archeological dig in Ethiopia in order to produce a first-rate narrative. The yardstick is not so much what they choose to write about, but how they present their subject. Dry, detailed summation is the enemy. Coach your students to avoid it at all costs.

Encourage students who are having difficulty finding a topic to make a list of all the activities they have pursued both in and out of school. They don't have to be sponsored activities necessarily. Any activity could have potential for an interesting essay, but students may not realize it at this stage.

In my role as an adjunct to the guidance department (working with students writing their college application essays), I often meet with seniors who have no idea of what topic they'd like to write about. My meetings with them begin with a confidential probe of their young lives. I try to get them thinking about possible topics and to help them see themselves in the backdrop of school, family, and society. This can be a difficult task: Ask ten teens about their passions, about what drives their lives, and it seems that nine of them will respond with a blank stare. High school students often perceive their lives as dull and boring. Nothing exciting ever seems to happen.

But when questioning them about their involvement in activities apart from school, I find their lives are anything but boring. They have a variety of jobs, both after school and during the summer. They volunteer in nursing homes and work with local officials to improve environmental concerns. They intern in hospitals. They have interesting hobbies and musical talents. They attend special camps and teen institutes. They tutor younger children.

Often it's not until they are questioned about items they have listed that students begin to realize that a topic has the potential to become an interesting read. Although successful authors provide conflicting advice—write about what you know, explore the unknown—it is best for young writers to write about an experience that has affected them personally.

However, school-related activities often do not lead to stellar essays. Not that they can't. It's just that students sometimes fail to see what would make the championship game, the NHS car wash, a Show Choir or Drama Club performance an interesting read. They usually get trapped in the chronological "and then" sequence of events.

When helping your students pick a topic, you can't emphasize enough that it's how the narrative unfolds that will carry the essay. What seems fascinating to the student, if told inexpertly, will not be interesting to the reader. Several college admissions officers report that the rehashing of sports injuries usually renders dull, dry accounts, mainly because the drama and excitement of the moment aren't relayed in a voice that seems unique to the individual student. If it could be anybody's broken arm or sprained ankle, then the reader won't remember anything about the person that actually sustained it.

Likewise, students that have visited Third World countries can produce ingenuous attempts at proving that the few weeks they spent in Guatemala enabled them to completely understand what it means to live in poverty. This type of essay is what Phyllis Supple, associate director of undergraduate admissions at Duke University, describes as "the epiphany, the ah-ha" essay. (Telephone interview, 18 September 2003). The danger of this type of narrative lies in the student focusing on broad issues with sweeping generalities.

When listing potential topics, students often shun situations that elicit frustration or disappointment for fear of appearing negative. Encourage them not to feel that way. I am finding each year that personal narratives often reveal the excessive emotional baggage that students carry to the classroom. They reflect more and more the poignant problems and concerns prevalent in our society today such as divorce, an abusive parent, teenage pregnancy, the suicide of a friend, battles with anorexia, a parent stricken with AIDS, etc. And I laud many writers who dealt with these wrenching accounts, for they wrote with candor and a sincerity that not only commanded respect from the reader but occasionally elicited legitimate compassion as well. Uyen's essay is one of these. She describes her father, a victim of Alzheimer's.

> *You sometimes come to me, sometimes as a vision on the periphery, scaling the edges of my eyes. Then there are times when I jerk around and catch sight of you, pulling an apple from the fridge, tucking a beer under your shirt, scratching a dry patch of skin. And I wonder, where did you go?*
>
> *I still remember the night you went away, so suddenly. I never had the chance to say goodbye. The night was firm from the coming autumn, crispy like a green granny apple. Outside the street was empty and dark save for the flowing sign of Bank One at the corner of the intersection. Usually we would be on the porch, watching fireflies flicker from the veil of darkness. You would be blowing puffs of smoke into the sky, catching stars with your breath. But that night you were inside, sprawled on the beige carpeting muddled with leasing contracts, license applications, and bills—the world on your back. A wasteland of beer cans and cigarette butts littered beside you, products*

of your grapple for "success." But no amount of wealth could have saved you that night…the night Atlas shrugged, sending my world into oblivion.

You left so suddenly, there was no time to pack. Your clothes still hung neatly in the closet, redolent with the odor of Marlboro and sweat, the scent of dreams gone up in smoke. When you used to wrap me in a hug, I would inhale your scent, thinking, "poor Daddy, poor, poor Daddy." Your shoes were still sitting on the mat, Vietnamese newspapers piled next to your bed, your black comb untouched in the drawer. But when you left, you took away my first report card, my sisters' names, our birthdays, our first steps, Khanh's blue ruffled dress, all the Christmases, New Years, dinners at Sizzler's, poses for pictures. You packed away the memories, you packed away your soul.

A stranger came to live with us after you left. He always asks my name. Some days I'm only eight and on his good days, I am about 15. He thinks I am clairvoyant because I can answer his questions before he even asks them. He doesn't remember that he has asked me them a million times before. We don't watch fireflies, and he doesn't catch stars at night. He scales the wall, a ghostly figure I sometimes forget exists. Then there are moments, rare moments when I catch flashes of you in him. Moments when I hear him laugh as we play dominos, when he translates "Paris by Night" into common Vietnamese for me to understand, when he smiles at the sight of my certificate in sixth grade signed by Bill Clinton. And I wonder, are you really gone?

Here's a list of topics that you can share with your students to help them realize that the potential for topics is enormous. These choices rendered interesting narratives in response to the "topic of choice" questions, where students revealed their interests and passions, their perceptions, values, reactions, and their ability to deal with the conflicts:

- working at a veterinarian office

- prepping dogs—and horses—for shows

- demonstrating how Monopoly evolved into a lesson in accepting defeat

- overcoming the fear of dogs

- going blank during a piano recital as a child, only to return to the stage with a successful performance as a teen

- enduring family moves—every other year

- developing an analogy comparing a course in European History to a football game

- coping with the pain of rheumatoid arthritis and learning to swallow 10 pills in a single swig

- enduring Outward Bound

- taking oceanography college courses while in high school

- having a father as a minister

- experiencing the Korean War Veterans Memorial for the first time

- working in a Chinese restaurant as a "renegade busboy"

- befriending a female resident in a nursing home who claimed to be a former CIA agent

- kindling a childhood friendship with a single call to China

- cutting off treasured braids and donating them to Locks for Love

- volunteering as a Little League coach, tennis coach, soccer coach

- volunteering in nursing homes, hunger centers

- working in a city's recreation department, city hall, amusement parks

- dealing with the challenges of being a twin

- being targeted repeatedly for random searches at airports

- owning an authentic Kate Spade purse

- dealing with laryngitis as the lead on opening night

- teaching piano to reluctant children

Conferencing

Again, I realize that individual conferencing may not be feasible for you as you struggle to meet all your classroom obligations. But I do want to remind you that conferencing is a powerful tool, and that even if individual meetings aren't possible, I hope you can find some method of conferencing to use with your students.

Conferencing can be helpful as early as topic selection. Students who are impassioned to write about a specific experience will usually begin their first drafts without intervention. But for those struggling to find a topic that will work, meeting with them briefly after they have composed a list of their activities can help them assess potential topics. I begin by questioning to scrutinize each item listed:

Is there one on the list that you feel passionate about?

Would you feel comfortable writing about it?

How did you get involved?

What positive and negative experiences did you have?

What was your reaction?

What did you learn from it?

How did it affect you?

How would you evaluate the experience?

Can you provide adequate examples and support given your choice?

Samples of Initial Conferences

Many students approach this initial conference sheepishly. When they submit their list of potential topics, they've already rationalized why most would not produce a good essay. My initial encouraging comments are often met with rebuke. "This is an interesting list," I'll say. "Yeah, but nothing exciting happened," the student says back. Further probing of their involvement with people and their reactions to the situations helps students to see the potential for an interesting essay. It did for Sam, Susan, and Kristen.

• Sam seldom spoke in class. His body language painted him as a disinterested individual who believed he could rely on his intelligence to maintain passing grades and usher him through any academic challenge. But then acceptance to the college of his choice was conditional, pending the quality of a supplemental essay he was requested to submit. This was a smack of reality for him and a surprise for me the day I found him in the writing center, eager to write a good narrative because of the pressure now burdening him. So we began. When I reviewed his meager list, I was again surprised—this time to find he had been volunteering at a nursing home for the past year. When I asked him to tell me about his experiences there, I got the expected teen-age response: "Nothing much happened." When I asked him to tell me specifically what he did during a typical visit, he said he transported patients to dinner. Exploring further, I found he had a card-playing routine after dinner with 90-year-old Charlie. From the tone of his voice I could tell Sam enjoyed listening to Charlie's stories of long ago.

As our dialogue continued, I began to see the person who sat passively in my class-room each day a bit differently. He had launched a card tournament with several residents. Poker was their game, and the ante was candy bars which Sam purchased every week. I suggested he use this experience as the topic of his essay. He agreed to pursue it. Days later, as I read through the wordy areas and misspellings of his first draft, I was touched by the description of how he felt when he learned Charlie died. While Sam persisted in camouflaging his emotions to appear "cool" before his classmates, he revealed in this essay that he was indeed a caring individual.

- Susan, on the other hand, had a long list of activities for her narrative, any one of which could have yielded an interesting essay. In our conference we focused on her visits to a hunger center. She said it was a good experience, but nothing she could write about. As I prodded her further, she told a dry tale about how her parish youth group class boarded the bus early one morning and what she saw when the group arrived in the inner city. Then she relayed the instructions she received for serving tables. "That's about it," she said.

But then I asked her how she had felt when she entered the center and what she had observed. After describing the food and the ramshackle building, she focused on the individuals waiting for their meal. That's when she exploded with latent anger. "It was awful," she said. "I went down there thinking I was doing a good deed and everyone would be thankful. But what I found was the complete opposite. The people were rude and offensive. One man even yelled at me for serving him a dessert he hated and threw the chocolate pudding at me."

As she continued, I listened intently, knowing this was an essay in the making. But she still did not recognize it. "Listen to what you're telling me," I prodded.

"I can't write about that!" she said. "It's all negative. I'll look like a terrible person."

"Or one who can deal with conflict by being perceptive and helpful?"

Susan learned that upbeat, pleasant approaches may not be effective if the writer is not communicating genuine reactions. Relating negative feelings can have great impact if the encounter is developed candidly and realistically.

- One of the most interesting conferences occurred with Kristen. She was vigorously athletic and when I saw she had listed her WSI (Water Safety Instruction), I asked her to tell me about some of her experiences. "Oh, nothing unusual," she said. "Lifeguarding can really be boring."

When asked about tennis camp, she told me how strenuous it was smashing ball after ball after ball in 100 degree weather, and how annoying it was to share the campus with teams of eighth grade boys attending soccer camp. We both agreed, not much of a story there...until I asked if anything unusual happened during her stay, if anyone got sick or injured. Immediately I saw a reaction in her brown eyes. "There was an incident last year." And she proceeded to tell her story.

Withering from the heat after hours of practice, she headed to the natatorium for relief only to find it swarming with aspiring soccer players. She was surprised to see that the two on-duty lifeguards were laughing and conversing with friends in a remote corner of the facility. This scenario foreshadowed the crisis that followed—she found a young boy at the bottom of the pool. I remember reading her essay for the first time as she related her panic and eventual success in saving the boy. But it didn't end with her portraying herself as a savior. What followed was a blustery attack on the irresponsible guards that reflected her deep sense of commitment and dedication. Kristen was a talented writer, yet for me her greatest asset was her humility—she had to be prodded to relate her heroism.
(You can read Kristen's essay beginning on page 89.)

In addition to discovering workable topics that they felt comfortable sharing, conferencing helped each of these students focus and narrow the details that they would use in their essays.

Brainstorming

In most English classes today teachers are using the writing process as a technique to help their students become better writers. The National Writing Project, first known as the Bay Area Writing Project, was established under the direction of James Gray in Berkeley, California in 1974, and has evolved into a nation-wide movement that brings teachers together in a unified approach to teaching writing. Who hasn't heard of "brainstorming," "clustering," and "revision"? And it's a process that makes sense. Providing students with specific steps helps to quell the frustration of how to begin, how to explore, and how to revise. It certainly communicates that writing is not a "one-shot deal." The process is a testimony to the premise that students (and teachers as well) become better writers because they write—and write often. Teachers who have participated in the NWP workshops can attest to the success of its basic principles. They practiced the process with colleagues—writing daily, sharing their work with their peers, recognizing that revision is an inherent part of writing and publishing. This approach can transform a classroom into an environment where writing is a very natural part of learning, where students discover and develop ideas while never relinquishing control of their writing.

The act of brainstorming—listing and clustering—can not only help students decide on their topic but also help them focus on an angle, a segment of the topic that can be developed fully. Every writer knows a chronological account of an event or situation will not retain a reader's attention. Having an angle will. It is that spin, that focus, that drives a piece of writing. The angle will help a personal narrative stay focused. Most students initially tend to scope an entire experience instead of selecting a portion and elaborating on it. Writing is a selective process and often students are so involved with the experience itself, they have difficulty eliminating the less important facts.

As students begin to brainstorm, they need to realize they will undoubtedly gather more information than they will actually use. Be sure to encourage them not to interrupt the flow of ideas or become too selective early in this gathering stage. Eventually, a two-fold process will be underway where they begin to eliminate extraneous information while elaborating on important points.

Clustering is a technique that helps students organize their thoughts and determine a sequential order—a road map—for their essay that will prevent them from digressing and straying off-topic. They can determine the sequential order of the main points of their essay before actually beginning to write. For example, Beth's essay on page 40 has four basic sections. It begins with the weary family's arrival in Slovakia, progresses to her purchase of the 59-cent McDonald's apple pie and the confrontation when it is stolen, and then concludes with her reactions to the incident.

Although you are familiar undoubtedly with the stages of the writing process, **Handouts #2 - #7** will facilitate your review of these initial steps with your students who need more structure throughout the prewriting process (selecting a topic, brainstorming, clustering, and determining the angle for the essay).

► HANDOUT #2 ◄

Beginning the Personal Narrative

Discovering your Topic ──► BRAINSTORMING

Some of you may immediately decide on a specific topic for your personal narrative and can begin brainstorming details pertaining to that topic. Others may have difficult choosing one. Listing your activities can help you select a topic.

What are your activities, interests, talents, hobbies, jobs, involvement with family, friends, nature, volunteering, etc.? List them below. Then examine your list. Which items appeal to you as a possible the topic for your essay?

Topic:

_____

HANDOUT #3

Brainstorming

Once you have chosen a topic, randomly jot down the items you recall about the experience or activity. Include brief details, examples, etc. Don't be selective at this stage. You should have more information gathered than you will use.

Topic: _____

Some considerations:

- brief background information

- individuals involved and their role

- your position and responsibility

- setting, location

- conflicts, their cause and effect

- your reactions, feelings

HANDOUT #4

Prewriting Practice

Brainstorm the topics listed below:

- a brother, sister, or relative

- a family trip or gathering

- your summer job

- an individual who has influenced you the most

- a challenging experience

Clustering

As you examine your brainstorming, you will see connections among some of the items listed. Using graphics such as lines, arrows, and circles will help you group or cluster items and begin to organize the content.

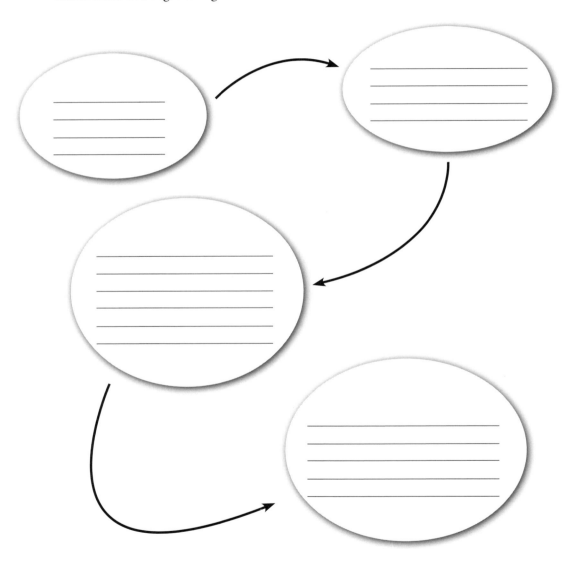

HANDOUT #6

Sample Clustering

Topic: Working in a fast-food restaurant

BACKGROUND

few summer jobs available
replaced a friend who quit
walked to interview in thunder storm
missed my ride
worked before at Chinese restaurant
served sit-down before

WHAT I LEARNED

be patient with customers
control temper
couldn't go out with friends
work schedule

people blamed me for their mistakes
they can't decide —don't read choices before
    coming to counter angered others behind
    them
held up line
friends wanted free food

CUSTOMERS

people in line rude and impatient
returned their orders uncooked
too greasy
wrong flavor drink
wrong order
changed their mind

working with others
be patient in meaningless interview
listen to manager
Never want to work behind a counter again!

CONDITIONS

crowded kitchen
hot-sticky
no tips
fast pace lunch & dinner time
minimum wage

HANDOUT #7

Discovering The Angle

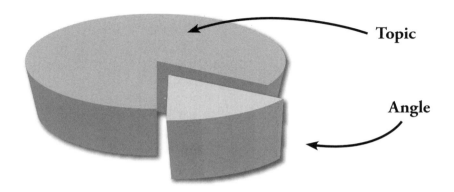

After clustering, consider a possible angle—that segment of the topic that you plan to pursue. It narrows the topic and becomes the focus of your essay. Including everything you have listed would produce a drawn-out, uninteresting essay—especially if all the facts are related chronologically.

In deciding upon your angle, you will be eliminating some information about your topic while elaborating on the items that will illustrate the angle.

1. What could be a possible angle for each of your brainstorming topics on Handout #4: a relative, family gathering, summer job, individual who has influenced you, a challenging experience?

2. What could be a possible angle for the fast-food clustering?
    (Handout #6)

3. Once you determine your angle, again list details, facts, descriptions, etc. that will help you develop it.

CHAPTER 4

Banging Out the First Draft

The biggest error students make when beginning a personal narrative is revising as they write. On-the-fly revision is inhibiting. It stifles the progression and development of ideas and harbors procrastination. Safely wallowing in the first paragraph of any piece of writing—correcting spelling errors, rewording unclear sentences, searching for more precise diction, etc.—allows writers to avoid grappling with the mix of details that convey meaning and create voice.

At this stage students would rather feed the iguana in the biology lab than write. All writers have indulged in procrastination—paying the bills, bathing the 100-pound pup, conversing with a telemarketer—anything to stall the intense labor. But writers simply have to bang it out without interruption. Tell your students that the first draft is a messy stage where writers need to ignore incomplete sentences and the nagging feeling that they have not found the appropriate word.

A good first draft is an oxymoron. It is often anything but good. It is not unusual for first drafts to be filled with incomplete ideas, unclear sentences, and clunky language. They are little more than roadmaps, sketches of the final product, call-backs for points that need to be expanded into completeness or whittled away for clarity. First drafts are often planted with symbols that designate awkward, unclear, or wordy areas that the author knows must be fixed.

Anne Lamott has been there and uses no euphemisms in describing her take on the first draft. In *Bird by Bird* she delightfully describes it as "shitty."

> "For me and most of the other writers I know, writing is not rapturous. In fact, the only way I can get anything written at all is to write really, really shitty first drafts.
>
> The first draft is the child's draft, where you let it all pour out and then let it romp all over the place, knowing that no one is going to see it and that you can shape it later. You just let this childlike part of you

channel whatever voices and visions come through and onto the page…"
(22-3).

Beginnings—First Impression of the "Story"

After they have hammered their way through their first drafts, encourage your students to evaluate their work for what shines, what needs to be deleted, and what needs more work. As they read, they need to keep in mind the importance of their opening statements. Encourage them to look for the most interesting moment in their first draft, and then to hone the material so that they can start as close to that moment as possible.

I encourage students to use what I call a grab-n-plop technique to get their personal narratives started: grab the readers' attention and plop them (*in medias res*) into the action immediately. As a classroom exercise, I often have students compare a chronological recount of getting to the final basketball game of the season ("we played Team X, and then Team Y, and almost lost to Team Z, but we pulled it out at the end") with a presentation of the action that takes place in the middle—or even at the end—of the final game of the season. Through description, sensory images, and development of the writer's reactions to other players, the audience, and the status of the team, readers can hear and see what happens both on the court and in the stands. I know students begin to understand the format when they ask, "You mean you want it to read like a story?"

Impress upon your students that unlike analytical writing, an expressive narrative does not require the traditional thesis statement in the introductory paragraph, nor does it require topic sentences as such. In fact, assure your students that the five-paragraph approach should not even be a consideration. It is too binding, too restrictive. I don't know if I should chuckle or cringe when I hear teachers at conferences confess to each other that they swear by the five-paragraph format for every essay. I declared it dead years ago, and thankfully my department agreed. Where is it written that a personal experience occurs within five paragraphs? Students need the freedom to unleash the angle that allows the paper to develop with continuity and culminate appropriately regardless of the number of paragraphs.

Avoiding the structure of the five-paragraph paper, however, is not an invitation to ramble on. Length is a factor with college essays. When admissions officers are enduring marathon reading sessions, they do not want excruciatingly long responses. Besides, many universities specify: No more than 500 words.

Each year students inevitably ask if they can use the first person in their personal narratives. They ask this as if they were seeking permission to ignore some written-in-stone axiom. "Of course you can!" I tell them. "It's your essay." The use of the pronoun "I" conveys an intimacy that can help grab readers and plop them into the story. Students' fear of using it usually stems from once having had a teacher who vehemently prohibited it.

Too often students are geared to pleasing you, the teacher, instead of venturing out independently for fear of failure. As they begin their personal narratives, encourage them to think of themselves not only as students but as fellow writers. As they work on their essays, they will learn first hand the struggle inherent in writing and eventually determine for themselves the countless decisions writers must make during the process. Students know that writing is hell. They just don't realize it's hell for everyone.

Student samples of first paragraphs are included in **Handout #8** on the CD. These demonstrate how the writers introduced their topics creatively with details and descriptions that draw the reader into the piece. Students are asked to share their reaction to each and discuss the techniques used to attract the reader's attention. **Handout #9** follows with brief commentaries explaining how the entire essay evolved from each of those beginning paragraphs.

HANDOUT #8

Opening Paragraphs

Read the following examples of opening paragraphs from various college essays. What is your reaction to each? How effective are these paragraphs in gaining the reader's attention?

1. *We were greeted at the door by the Abbot, a man who upon initial examination more closely resembled a '70's disc jockey than greater Cleveland's answer to Friar Tuck. Grinning warmly behind his yellow-tinted glasses and goatee, he told us where to drop our sizeable cardboard boxes and offered to take us on a tour of the premises before he put us to work.*

   Luke

2. *The chill, unyielding tile floor—the soft moan of a crackling radio playing throughout the empty aisles—I'm alone at my video store job, and it seems as though the entire world belongs to me. Outside, the parking lot reflects the solitary feeling that has begun to set in. Inside, the absence of footsteps sounds even louder than the normal scuttle of movie browsers. Suddenly every nerve in my body is*

raging, and my hands counting the $20 bills under the counter are trembling to such an extent that one single paper bill flutters to the floor. As I bend to retrieve it, I wonder when I became so aware of the cruel possibilities of the world around me.

Amy

3. *As I look in the mirror, my appearance seems incomplete. I seem fine: all facial features intact, feet still moving, bones in place. Nevertheless, my exterior lacks the sparkle of my childhood days. Intently, I gaze at my thick hair, which bears a shade resembling auburn. Reminiscing, I long for the days when my hair was bright red.*

Matt

4. *What do you picture when you hear the words "Little League Baseball?" Do you see happy, whimsical little kids? Children running around a baseball diamond with gleeful faces? I did, too, but that all changed the day I became a Little League coach.*

Craig

5. *I shuffle across the dirt road, breathing in the warm air, the sweet smell of the jasmine blossoms lingering through the smell of cow dung. A young woman, about 15 stands at the entrance to the schoolhouse, and her shy smile broadens in response to my own grin. She begins to bow respectfully, but I stop her halfway down. I bend slightly to peer into her eyes. They are frightened now; all the warmth and joy have vanished. I speak softly, cajolingly in Tamil. "You needn't bow to me. We are equals, you and I."*

Sonia

6. *Where have all the gypsies gone? As in the days of yore, they still travel trodden pathways through forests, weeded fields, farms and backyards—secretive, out of the "nine to five" world, always seeking anonymity, treasures and truth. No longer are there wooden wagons adorned with festively hued bric-a-brac and cluttered with the wares of nomadic existence—pots, pans and vibrant draperies. But the often-secluded camps still endure, attended by drifters donning motley layers of mismatched clothing, trinkets, watches on fobs, bandanas, and hats with rims perforated by badges from exotic places. To me, these gypsies have become the everyday norm, for I have grown up surrounded by their eccentricities and uncommon characteristics, unique to each. Perhaps, "gypsy" may*

not be the most descriptive word for this clan. Maybe I should refer to them as a menagerie of wanderers, a family derived from several families or more precisely, an archeology crew.

Lynne

▶ HANDOUT #9 ◀

Comments on the Opening Paragraphs

1. Luke's subtle humor, which immediately endears him to his reader, is captured in his unique and vivid imagery. From his initial impression of the abbot, comparing him to a would-be Friar Tuck and a '70's disc jockey, the reader is drawn into the volunteer drive to deliver food and products to a church.

2. Annie's description and sensory images help to communicate her anxiety and create the atmosphere that was the backdrop of a late night incident she experienced. She was working at a video store and an irrational, intrusive male warned her that she was a prime candidate for rape or even homicide. "The cruel possibilities of the world around me" leads the reader into that incident.

3. Lacking the anxiety of Annie's paragraph, Matt's beginning communicates a humorous spin on having had red hair as a child. The essay later builds to a shocking reality when he learns during a childhood visit to the Natural History Museum that "red heads are those most likely to go bald!"

4. The reader may assume from the last sentence of Craig's opening paragraph that his experience as coach would not be a delightful one, yet his questioning tone hints that it will be a humorous romp of challenging experiences. And so it was. Describing one of the little players in his essay, he states: "This (kid) would have been able to convince anyone he was a Keebler Elf with his innocent mop of blond hair and goofy grin. But behind that grin was a virulent spirit." Craig was candid throughout and acknowledged his lack of success—the group never did become a team. Despite his efforts they simply

remained fourteen individual players and two coaches.

5. Sonia's opening statement establishes the atmosphere of the
    rural area with the juxtaposition of sweet jasmine blossoms
    and cow dung. Her encounter with Sharma, the girl at the
    schoolhouse, reflects the poverty in India that prevents children
    from pursuing an education and also demonstrates the respect
    accorded teachers. She did manage to enroll Sharma in school,
    but not without first speaking to her parents and opening her
    home to her. Sonia's essay ended with a single quote: "Sharma,
    this is the letter 'A.'" And so began Sharma's education.

6. Lynne's opening questions lead the reader to believe that she
    is describing traditional gypsies in a modern setting. Her
    travelers cross "trodden pathways" but they have abandoned
    their "wooden wagons adorned with festively hued bric-a-brac
    and cluttered with wares of nomadic existence—pots, pans and
    vibrant draperies." She allows the reader's belief to continue
    until she redefines these wanderers and explicitly identifies
    them in the final two words.

You have probably read student papers that recount experiences by overworking a
single aspect of an incident, making readers feel that they are wandering aimlessly
toward some eventual message or point. Other essays may provide abundant factual
information but lack the description that keeps the writing from being flat and
uninviting. **Handout #10** presents two students whose opening paragraphs provide
a distinct contrast: one suffers from a loss of perspective and the other is clearly
defined but totally emerged in facts.

Ericson

Ericson's topic was to evaluate a significant experience, achievement, risk, or ethical
dilemma he had endured and to discuss its impact on him. His first account was
steeped in generalizations. It focused on the philosophy of decision making and the
effect of choices that individuals make. This lengthy build-up delayed introducing
a terrifying, but compelling incident that occurred while he and his family were
camping on the rocky coast of the Georgian Bay.

The cause of the accident (which resulted in the senseless loss of a life) had affected
Ericson greatly. The individuals involved had been drinking and had dared one of
their companions to jump off the highest cliff on the coast. The victim could not

contend with the high winds or roaring surf and died instantly upon reaching the water. Despite Ericson's attempt to get help, the victim could not be saved.

After I read his original paragraph, I listened to Ericson discuss the incident. He shared the first moments of the scene he had witnessed—the screams, the bodies plunging into the water attempting to save the victim—and his initial panic, his drive to seek help, and the impact the incident had on him. Verbally he sequenced the incident in a format that would elicit an interesting account, one that would certainly keep the reader's interest throughout.

"Listen to what you're telling me," I told him. "What would happen if you reorganized your essay so you described the scene first—your determination to get help—and then talked about the effect it had on you?"

"Yeah," he said. "Why didn't I think of that?"

"You did," I responded. "Just now, verbally. So go do it, and then we'll compare your first draft with the revised one. But then **you** will have to decide which one you should use."

Needless to say, Ericson's revised version was quite an improvement. He felt the *in medias res* beginning would attract readers immediately and provide them with a memorable surrogate experience. The restructuring also helped to improve his style of writing: it became more concise, descriptive, and focused. He still had an abundance of subject-verb sentence structures, but in the revised version they functioned to build momentum, whereas in the first draft, they had only contributed to his rambling.

Ben

Ben is a sensitive, unassuming young man. This is apparent the first time you meet him. But he is also an individual with strong convictions. During our first conference I knew he was committed to his topic. His account of his participation as a member of the American delegation to Seeds of Peace (a multi-cultural camp involving 200 teens from Israel, Palestine, Egypt and Jordan) revealed how passionate he felt about his involvement. A realist as well, Ben knows that an international camp tucked away in Maine will not quell the turbulence and strife in the Middle East today, but he perceives the potential for coexistence to open the channels for peace as a reality.

A talented writer, Ben introduced his topic in his first draft clearly and concisely. It was a solid approach. Yet as we talked and he began to describe the people and events he experienced, his reserve began to wane as he described some of the emotionally charged incidents he experienced. Realizing that his opening paragraph was factual and lacked a voice that would draw the reader to the camp, he decided to rewrite the beginning by focusing on descriptions and citing specific examples.

Handout #10 on the CD asks students to read the question both Ericson and Ben addressed. The first paragraphs are their original attempts, the second, their revised versions. Students are asked to read both sets and discuss their reactions while providing support for their rationale.

▶   # HANDOUT #10   ◀

Revised Opening Paragraphs

Both Ericson and Ben address the following question: "Evaluate a significant experience, achievement, risk you have taken, or ethical dilemma you have faced and its impact on you." Read both sets of opening paragraphs and discuss your reaction to each. Be sure to provide specific examples in support of your rationale.

Ericson

Original:

> *We, as human beings, interact with the world around us through the experiences that we go through, and the choices that we make in regard to these experiences. These choices that we make can effect our lives in many different ways, ending with either positive or negative outcomes. The world would be a perfect place if the decisions that we make could always have a positive outcome, but this is sadly not always the case. Sometimes, though, we have the ability to change a bad decision that we have made into a learning experience with a positive outcome. Other times, a bad decision can be so devastating that changing it into something positive is not even an option. Every day people are given challenges, opportunities, and problems in their lives that they will need to make decisions on. There is no other alternative to get around this simple form of reality. In order for us to interact with the world around us and to survive, we will need to make choices. These choices that we make can be big or small, but the one factor [that] will always remain is the decision, whatever it may be, [that] will have to be made. In my life, I have made many decisions. Some of these choices have been good, and others have been bad. I have also witnessed many decisions being made by the people surrounding me in my life. No matter who has made the decision, I have always*

tried to learn something from what the outcome of that decision may have been. In doing this, I have tried to teach myself to make the right choices, and steer clear of the wrong ones. I have had one experience in my life that has impacted me more than anything to make the right decisions.

Revised:

His limp body rose to the surface of the water for a brief moment, only to sink back as if being pulled by the black nothing below. Screams were heard from the cliff above as two more bodies plunged into the water. Time stood still as the bay grew quiet, but the silence quickly ended as three tiny heads emerged from the crashing waves. Two figures were carrying a body that appeared as if life itself had been left behind, under the dark blue water. The men lifted the limp body onto a ledge, just high enough to keep them safe from the crushing waves below. The body lay on the cold hard rocks motionless, as the other two tried breathing life back into him. Every attempt made, failed. Further help was essential but stood ninety-five feet above on the edge of a cliff. These people above could only stare down the rocky wall. They could only watch the wind push ten feet waves into the side of the ledge as if the water wanted back what it had claimed. On that ledge stood two men doing everything in their power to revive their friend, but something more had to be done. The doctors that could properly help this young man had to be reached, but they sat four miles away, oblivious to the events that were taking place. When this was realized, a young boy took off running as if hell itself was chasing right behind him. With all the strength of a ten-year-old boy, he knew he was running for someone who desperately needed help. This little boy was me.

Ben

Original:

In 1993, a renowned journalist and author named John Wallach suggested something that few others involved in the Middle East conflict dared to suggest: he wanted to bring together Israeli, Palestinian, Egyptian and Jordanian teens together to coexist for three weeks at a camp in Maine. Fifty years of sporadic violence, thousands of deaths, and a deeply rooted hatred between Jews and Arabs did not stop Wallach's dream from becoming a reality, and in the summer of 1993, the Seeds of Peace family was born. In 2001 I joined the family as part of the American delegation to Seeds of Peace International Camp and had three of the most fascinating, difficult, compelling, and surely influential weeks of my life.

Revised:

> *To my right, Israeli and Palestinian flags flew side by side, surrounded by Egyptian, Jordanian, Tunisian and Qatari flags. These flags represented nations in which conflict was the norm, violence, a permanent wall preventing progress on the path to peace, and death not always front-page news. For three weeks each summer, Seeds of Peace (SOP) allows 200 teenagers from these nations to see the human face of their enemies and to wipe away the hatred that has blinded them from a vision of peace. I stepped back from the microphone after speaking on behalf of the 20 American campers who had come to Maine to act as bridges among enemies. A brown-eyed Israeli girl complimented my speech and a tall Arab boy put his arm over my shoulders. I realized that I was standing in probably the only place in the world where a Palestinian flag stood next to an Israeli flag. Emotionally touched, and determined to play a part in bringing peace to the world, a lone tear crept down my cheek as we walked into the camp gates under the green SOP flag.*

Body of the Essay

Anyone who teaches writing knows that ideas cannot exist in isolation. Moving from the opening paragraph into the body of the essay requires a coherent and sequential development of the angle in a series of paragraphs. To ensure the essay will evolve coherently, transitions are crucial. They are the "connectors" that help the narrative evolve smoothly from paragraph to paragraph. They are also the vital links within paragraphs as they connect ideas. Often as teachers we find ourselves qualifying the nature of transitions in personal narratives because generally they are not as stringently used as they are in analytical essays and articles. Their subtlety helps to sustain the writer's voice and flow of language.

In the following essay Beth discusses a traumatic incident she encountered in Slovakia. She manages not to use intrusive transitions yet still controls the sequential development of the episode. The reference to "Kosice's melted ice cream ambiance" at the end of the first paragraph functions as a segue into the McDonald's purchase and foreshadows the pending conflict. The mention of the "this potentially dangerous situation" at the beginning of the third paragraph is a transition linking it to the previous paragraph with the girl rushing towards her. As the "American apple pie" incident unfolds, a realization surfaces in the fifth paragraph: "Why didn't I recognize her hunger?" This personal chiding lingers into the last paragraph as Beth is haunted by her instinctive reaction to save the pie.

> *We were train-weary in the city of harsh modernization and cold gray cement: Kosice, Slovakia. My parents and I were tired from sleeping in overpriced hotels like*

the Ranc, a hotel with cowboy bedspreads and Marlboro ads tacked to the walls. We were tired of paying dour old women 20 koruns to use the public restrooms. Here tall gray stacks of Soviet block apartments with sad laundry drooping out of the windows separated the city from the fields of sunflowers that I had enjoyed blur past me on the train. The welcome from military officials armed with guns and muzzled dogs when the train from Poland pulled into the station was the beginning of Kosice's melted ice cream ambiance.

Not surprisingly, the cashier in the city's McDonald's did not volunteer her English to help me order. After pantomiming the licking of an ice cream cone, I pointed to the row of apple pies lined up on stainless steel behind her. With both of my snacks in hand, I headed back to the train station, our temporary home until the six o'clock train to Budapest arrived. Immediately after looking up from my dripping cone in one hand and the pocket-sized apple pie in the other, I made eye contact with a girl my age rushing at me. I wish I could say that I caught her intense face, her seedy eyes. I was only left with the image of her dark figure steadily walking toward me.

The unusual element about this potentially dangerous situation was that I did not feel threatened. I felt like laughing in her determined face. I was 15. She didn't knock me to the cement, nor did she pull out a knife from her layers of clothing, nor did she grab my purse and run. Instead, she snatched my apple pie.

I refused to let go of my purchase—my American apple pie. We started twisting in a circle, both gripping half of that worthless pie, and I remember reprimanding, screaming at her in English, "I paid for this! Who taught you to steal?" No one on that crowded lot stopped to break up the struggle or at least to watch the winding dance of a tattered girl and a young American traveler.

In resignation, she ripped it through its cardboard container and ran with half of it. She left me with apple filling oozing down my arm. On the way back to the station, looking over my shoulder, I licked tears of melted vanilla, sweet as sin. I kept wondering why she didn't seize my purse. **She stole my food.** I should have offered to take her to McDonald's and buy her a happy meal. Why didn't I recognize her hunger?

I think about this girl. I'll be sitting in the theater sharing a tub of popcorn with a row of friends, or setting my family's dining room table with organized rows of gleaming forks and knives, and I try to imagine her face. I think about my life, my tubs of popcorn, my meticulous rows of silverware. I think about my dad's chicken curry on Sundays, my grandma's steaming pots of noodle soup carried home from weekends away, and gingersnaps folded in wax paper and delivered to my grandpa. I try to picture a time when I was a 15-year-old girl, selfishly hoarding a 59-cent American apple pie.

Handout #11 on the CD reviews the function of transitions, and **Handout #12** illustrates how transitions can be used between paragraphs and within a single paragraph in Michael's Alien Ant Farm review for his high school newspaper.

HANDOUT #11

The Function of Transitions

According to
In addition to
Also
Beyond
Furthermore
First, second, etc.
→ **provide additional facts**

Although
In contrast
However
Even though
On the other hand
But, yet
Instead of
→ **present a contrast, another viewpoint**

Then
Meanwhile
Afterwards
Next
While
→ **provide a sequence of time**

Therefore
Because
As a result
Since
→ **show cause/effect**

▶   HANDOUT #12   ◀

Transitions as Links

Transitions can be used between paragraphs and within a single paragraph as well. Michael wrote a review of Alien Ant Farm for his high school newspaper. His transitions helped to connect his views while comparing the group's two albums.

Alien Ant Farm almost had their career as a band cut short when their tour bus **crashed** in the back of a semi in Spain…

Although the accident nearly paralyzed their lead singer…and injured the rest of the band, it did not deter Alien Ant Farm from…unleashing their second album.

TruANT includes the same type of catchy riffs and hooks…released on ANThology, **but** the band expanded upon the depth of the songs…

Aside from a few insignificant short-comings, Alien Ant Farm released a formidable album in TruANT. Fans of ANThology must buy the album. **However**, if the first album did not suit your musical tastes, don't waste any time listening to this album. This band has a sound they like and they're sticking to it.

Concluding Paragraphs

Unlike the closing paragraph in an analytical essay, which restates the thesis or summarizes the results of researching a topic, the end of a narrative essay often provides creative closure. It, too, can summarize in a brief paragraph, but it might also conclude with just a clincher that capitalizes on the distinct voice present throughout the essay. A talented writer with a never-ending quest to learn, Justin's essay below reflects simple yet sustaining conclusions.

Those who are unfamiliar with an instrument such as the piano will stare at sheet music with a mixture of intimidation and awe, intimidation at the intricate patterns of black dots and sweeping lines and foreign symbols as incomprehensible as Sanskrit, and awe at the ability to transform at a whim what is already a work of art on the printed page into art of auricular form: the grand weaving of melodies and harmonies and soaring choruses and jarring dissonance and their ultimate resolution.

Marks on paper, however beautiful, fail to capture the nature, the spontaneity of music. Ink on paper is stagnant while notes in music are ephemeral, the birth and death of each note spanning no longer than the fraction of a moment, its fleeting essence lasting just long enough to be perceived and impressed upon the mind. While an author captures the spirit of his or her imagination within the pages of a novel, confining impalpable ideas and transient images within a cage skillfully wrought of nouns, adjectives, and verbs, a composer sets the essence of his creativity free, projecting these ideas and images into the world through ethereal sound.

Esoteric scribbles on the leaves of a compilation of sheet music are not in themselves the acclaimed works of art, the masterpieces. One can analyze the <u>Well-Tempered Clavier</u> just as one can analyze <u>Paradise Lost,</u> but one cannot appreciate the elegant beauty of Bach's creation through printed symbols as one can Milton's. In sheet music, the patterns of ink are a mere representation, a wire-frame model of what must be sculpted, fleshed out, and given hue and life by the performer.

The gift of the musician is part black magic and part alchemy; it is the ability to bestow life upon the inanimate, to transmute leaden ink to golden sound. Every concert, every recital of a piece is an act of creation. Every performance is the birth of an original piece of art. Pianists all over the world play the <u>Fantaisie Impromptu</u>, but each performance, like the performer, is unique. When one performs, one captures the verve and passion for music from the depths of one's soul, imbuing them with life and substance. It is this creation, this enrichment of my world that I revel in.

Creation—the development, evolution, and application of one's thoughts and ideas, is mankind's most precious ability. One who does not create merely inhabits the world, pushed along by the tides of Fate, not adding but only subtracting from humanity, stagnating rather than progressing. Only those who create leave their mark upon the world. Only they have the privilege of gazing backwards over the road of Time, pointing to a landmark in the distance, and stating with pride, "That was mine."

Remind your students that the goal of their first draft is to develop material that will allow them to find their essays' angle. As they work through this early stage, they must capture their random thoughts and prepare them for assembly into a sequential flow of thought. This is a complex process, yet is a very important stage in the development of an essay.

Once the draft harnesses the points that explain and support the angle, the writer can sigh a moment of relief before they begin the process of refining. A good place to start the revision process is with the voice of the narrative. A well-written essay is driven by an engaging voice that welcomes readers and lures them to continue reading to the very end. And that is one of the most difficult elements of writing to master. Chapter 5 addresses techniques to help students become aware of the power of voice in their writing.

CHAPTER 5

Voice

I don't believe voice can be *taught* as such. Voice is that quality that evolves naturally from within the heart of a writer much like music arises from the soul of the concert pianist. Creating a strong written voice is—as Justin describes the art of the musician in his essay at the end of Chapter 4—"part black magic and part alchemy." A writer's voice allows written words to paint an aural image, a transcript of personal experience that, when read, recreates the teller's spoken voice. It evolves (in part) from the nuances of word patterns, descriptions and details, diction, intonation, syntax, hyperbole, and understatement.

Voice, with its ability to capture the human spectrum of emotions, is definitely a major component of any strong personal narrative. Offer your students the opportunity to practice its development. It will make them better writers in general and will certainly prepare them to write strong college application essays in their junior and senior years.

Modeling the ways that professional writers develop voice in nonfiction, poetry, and drama—and allowing your students to discuss the effectiveness of voice in each other's pieces during peer sharing—will demonstrate the power voice can play in their own writing.

Handout #13 on the CD provides guidelines for students to help them not only hear but also listen to the verbal sounds that surround them daily. It highlights the components of written voice as well.

HANDOUT #13

Tuning in to Voice

Voice reflects your personality. It gives life to your essay. It holds your reader's attention and moves them through the piece. In well-written narratives the reader will "hear" you say what you're writing.

Here are some components of spoken voice that you should pay attention to when composing a written voice:

- rate of the spoken word
- pitch and intonation of the voice as it rises and falls
- rhythm of word patterns
- syntax
- diction, description and details

- Train yourself to listen to how other people speak. How does spoken language reflect their emotions, reactions, and mood? What happens when they speak rapidly versus slowly and deliberately? What effect does the pitch of their voice have? How do people use description when talking about others, when relating an incident, or when describing a particular locale? Note the way people use exaggeration in speech. What does hyperbole do to their voices?

- Throughout the day, listen to yourself speak. Note the **rhythm** and chords of your language—your **intonation** and the **rate** of your speaking voice. What is the effect when you exaggerate syllables or words with a higher pitch? What happens when you accelerate and slur your words in rapid succession? Increasing your rate of speech can reflect exhilaration, excitement, even fear, anger, or impatience. Decreasing the rate of speech can be used to emphasize a point or demonstrate grief, uncertainty, or worry. Analyze the diction and sound patterns of slang expressions like "duh" where a single expression can communicate light sarcasm.

- These variations of patterns can be reflected in your writing as well. This is the power of **syntax,** the arrangement of words and word patterns in sentences which can create a multitude of effects. For example, short subject-verb sentences can build momentum or indicate anger. Long, flowing sentences can capture a pleasant atmosphere or provide explanations. Repetition of words can emphasize uncertainty, the need to rationalize, or it can demonstrate an emphatic stand.

Within syntactical patterns the varying use of punctuation also helps to communicate voice. Dashes, for example, can be used for interruptions or brief digressions which closely imitate speech. They also can indicate a person's hesitation to act or the crashing reality of an unpleasant situation. Exclamation points can anchor the irony in a statement or an emphatic declaration. (A word of caution: Use them sparingly.)

- Just as the spoken voice can vividly recreate an emotion, scene, or experience, so too can the written voice. The life-line for good writing lies in the quality of the **description, details**, and unique **imagery**. These can reproduce a scene or event while communicating your tone and attitude. They can highlight your humor, sarcasm, whimsical approach, or anguish.

Techniques to Help Students Tune In to Voice

As a department chair I was at times approached by colleagues who were frustrated in their attempts to help students recognize an author's voice in fiction, drama, and especially in poetry. But more, they were searching for models and exercises that would demonstrate the connection between the spoken voice and the written voice. In addressing this challenge, I began to think of the ways that language impacts our daily lives. Listed below are some of the options I pursued that were successful.

To help students identify the components of voice, encourage them to listen to the live language they hear daily—the personal conversation with a friend, the one-sided cell phone conversations heard in public places, the collage of conversations in the lunch room, the conference with a teacher, the cheering at games. Ask them to listen to the ways they speak to their parents, to their pet.

Voices are seldom delivered in a monotone. The pitch of a speaking voice reflects a range of tonal fluctuations that can illustrate humor, sadness, euphoria, sarcasm, anger, etc. Every day, students are bombarded with verbal sounds in the halls, at concerts, at parties. They can *hear* the din of noise surrounding them, but they generally are not trained to *listen* to the fluctuations of voice.

Encourage students to observe how body language communicates as well, for it physically punctuates a person's voice. Consider the pounding fist or the pointed finger, the gyrations of extended arms and the hands covering tears of disappointment. Occasionally in class, discussing voice, I would shout, "Freeze. Don't move!" Since I had my students sit in a half circle, it was easy to select extreme examples of body language and ask students to describe their reactions to Mr. Cool, slumped down in his chair with outstretched legs crossed at the ankles and arms bent across his chest or Miss Frizzy with her finger captured in her tightly entwined curls—both steeped in apparent boredom. Adjectives would flood the room describing the frozen postures.

Sometimes I would show clips from the following movies to demonstrate how body language can complement voice:

> *Breakfast Club*
> *Forest Gump*
> *Good Will Hunting,*
> *Meet Joe Black*
> *Much Ado about Nothing*
> *The Sixth Sense*
> *Stand by Me*

In much the same way that a speaker's body language shares information about meaning, writers can include quick descriptions of people and physical objects to augment voice as it is developed through syntax, rhythm, and description.

Other Activities to Help Students Hear the Sounds of Language

- Read to them in class. They may be teenagers, but they still enjoy listening to a good essay or story. You may want to consider passages from these sources:

  > *Bird by Bird*, Anne Lamott
  > *The Bluest Eye*, Toni Morrison
  > *The Bonesetter's Daughter,* Amy Tan
  > *Caramelo*, Sandra Cisneros
  > *The Faith of a Writer,* Joyce Carol Oates
  > *House on Mango Street,* Sandra Cisneros
  > "I Have a Dream," Martin Luther King Jr.
  > *Nine Horses,* Billy Collins
  > *On the Rez,* Ian Frazier
  > *The Poisonwood Bible,* Barbara Kingsolver
  > *Sailing Alone Around the Room,* Billy Collins
  > *The Samurai's Garden,* Gail Tsukiyama
  > *The Secret Life of Bees,* Sue Monk Kidd
  > "Shooting an Elephant," George Orwell
  > *Small Wonder,* Barbara Kingsolver

To Kill a Mockingbird, Harper Lee

Woe Is I, Patricia O'Conner

Wouldn't Take Nothing For My Journey Now, Maya Angelou

Writers live in their voice. It's their livelihood. It's what lures the reader into the created realm of adventure, romance, conflict, mystery, passionate appeals for social change, humorous responses to life's absurdities. These modern voices continue to touch their readers:

Russell Baker	Thomas Friedman	Adrienne Rich
Dave Barry	Ellen Goodman	William Safire
Wendell Berry	Jamaica Kincaid	Susan Sontag
Bill Bryson	John McPhee	John Updike
Joan Didion	Jane Pauley	
Annie Dillard	Anna Quindlen	

- Have your students listen to and discuss the lyrics of songs.

- Play recordings of writers reading their essays and stories. National Public Radio offers several programs.

- Play the CD's included in *Poetry Speaks*: *Hear Great Poets Read Their Work from Tennyson to Plath.* This is an anthology of poetry that includes three audio CD's of poets reading their works. The edition also provides commentaries about the poems and poets presented in the book by writers such as Seamus Heaney, Billy Collins, and Rita Dove. Many refer to the sounds of the poems. For example, Richard Wilbur says about Robert Frost's poetry "… the sounds and rhythms of his poems were to echo or evoke the natural intonations of animated speech" (48).

Nancy Willard, a lecturer at Vassar College, provides insight that touches the conscientious heart of every English teacher. In *Poetry Speaks* she says,

> "When people ask me, 'How do you teach poetry?' I say, 'Start by giving your students a poem that speaks to them in so clear and astonishing a voice they might carry it with them for the rest of their lives.' This makes me feel like a doctor dispensing prescriptions for an underfed imagination. Take two poems by Denise Levertov, to be read at bedtime. No limit on refills." (270)

- Jump-in readings beckon students to participate in reading works aloud in class without being called upon. Sheridan Blau, senior lecturer at the University of California, Santa Barbara, and former president of NCTE, discusses this technique in his book *The Literature Workshop: Teaching Texts and Their Readers.* One student starts to read from the beginning of a work and anyone, at any time, can jump in either at the end of a paragraph or at a "natural stopping point" to continue the reading (128). No hands are raised, no nervous anticipation of being called upon. As more and more students participate, the reading takes on a unique and interesting spin because so many intonations and interpretative voices are heard. I have used this approach with essays, poetry, drama, and fiction, and the students enjoy the freedom and the various interpretations that are heard.

Relaxing Grammar to Create Voice

Having students read modern essays helps them to understand not only how powerful written language can be but also how to relax grammar rules in order to accomplish a distinct voice. Though some readers may quake at the thought of condoning sentences that begin with *and* or *but,* splitting an infinitive for emphasis, or using contractions to capture the casual flavor and voice of a piece, these digressions from traditional grammar are respectable today when establishing a conversational voice in essays. If this destroys my credibility, I strongly suggest you read Barbara Kingsolver's *Small Wonder.* When a newspaper asked her to write a response to 9/11, she was stimulated to write essay after essay in which she captured many vignettes of her life in an engaging personal style filled with contractions and conversational tone. Or read Patricia O'Conner's *Woe Is I* where she challenges English teachers who shudder at contraction sightings. Or William Zinsser's *On Writing Well* which takes on the stodgy use of semicolons. On the other hand, Lynne Truss, a British writer and journalist, counters any attempt at eliminating semicolons. In fact, she emphatically defends their use in her best-seller *Eats, Shoots & Leaves* and delightfully sanctions her reader to love punctuation.

True, all writers need to be aware of traditional grammar and know when it's appropriate to slip in and out of its hold. Students must be aware of the formality of our language when addressing standardized tests, submitting resumes, etc. But they also must realize that relaxing their grammar, particularly when writing personal essays, is acceptable since doing so reels in their reader with patterns that echo our modern language. If writing is taught exclusively "by the book," student writing will evolve stilted and stiff. Our purpose, then, is to expose students to the realities of our ever-changing language and to help them adapt it to accommodate better the purpose of each writing assignment.

Handout #14 provides examples of student narratives and instructs the reader to analyze how the writers sustain voice when disclosing their personal experiences and personalities.

▶ # HANDOUT #14 ◀

Voice in Student Narratives

Read the following samples of student essays and consider how the writers sustain their voice while disclosing their personal experiences and personalities.

1. Leah's profile is captured in stardust and those extra bones that juxtapose her liberal views with her theatrical belief in fairies. How is her voice developed and sustained throughout?

> *I have three extra bones in my right foot. I do, right on the bottom of my big toe. Most people have 206 bones in their body. I have 209. But beyond that, I guess I'm pretty ordinary. I live in an upper middle class, conservative town. You could say I don't really fit in since I'm incredibly liberal. I believe gay marriages should be legal. I believe that American citizens have the right to burn the flag. I believe in a women's right to choose—and I believe in fairies. From the moment I saw my first play,* Peter Pan, *and the great lights dimmed while the orchestra fashioned its melodic phrases, I had fallen in love with the enchantment of theatre. My heart flew out of my chest as Peter soared through the nursery window; my insides flinched at the sight of the peg-legged, black toothed, one-eyed pirates, and my hands rapidly pounded together as Peter asked us if we believed in fairies. And I did, I truly believed in fairies.*
>
> *From that moment on, I lived in a magical, eccentric, dynamic, unconventional, beautiful world known as theatre. Fall leaves weren't reddish. They were auburn. Time wasn't built on hours and seconds. Time was a series of delightful and charming moments. I could never understand how people could see raindrops and not wish to be outside splashing and singing in a lemon-colored raincoat and cap.*
>
> *I wish on stars in a world where stars are just bundles of gas. I dream in colors not yet invented in a world that dismisses dreamers. I am surprised by something everyday in a world that's taken for granted. I stop at every Crayola-colored poster lemonade stand and pay a dollar for a 25-cent Dixie Cup filled with one part lemon and 10 parts sugar water—all in a world that forgot how to make lemonade out of*

lemons. And still, I believe in fairies. So I guess I'm just like everyone else, perhaps a bit more eccentric and colorfully out of place. But how could you expect anything less from a girl with three extra bones?

2. Melvin is confronted with the task of writing his college essay that must be restricted to one page. What is the tone of his essay?

> *I could write an essay, if I wanted to. It would be spectacular—the story of my life with drama, love, heroism, a masterpiece to stand the test of time like a pillar against the desert sands. Metaphors, anaphora, zeugma would be the tools at my disposal to intertwine syntax and style. I know what I must do: I will write one. Now, where to begin. Oh, yes, of course.*
>
> *One wonders what marvels inhabit the adolescent mind still awake at 4:03 a.m. After two cups of coffee, and zero conscious hours devoted to staring at a collection of lines and curves assembled in parallel fashion to the paper's edge, I conclude that nothing resides in the mind of a high school student at this hour. Indeed…I have begun to fancy insanity or at least the inevitable euphoria born from sleep deprivation and Maxwell House. Nonetheless I continue to work.*
>
> *How will I begin? Will I open with birth? Will I use a clever anecdote about my days as a six-year-old backup for the team's reserve batter? Will short, well-written sentences about my captivating days as a paper boy hook the reader like a struggling guppy caught in the chains of merciless men? Perhaps I will draw pictures. But alas, no, I cannot.*
>
> *The monitor laughs at me with a black stare. I have finished but one sentence…suddenly I have found an idea. I will write about my days as a ballroom dancer floating across the polished floor with long sweeping glides—box step, one and two and three, box step, one and two and three.*
>
> *I will reminisce about the cheerful days of cha-cha-cha and the crescent moons of tango. I will make my cast of words dance, swinging in perfect unison to the trumpets of a jazz band. I will love my essay as a progeny of my inner-self.*
>
> *Only one problem remains: How will I fit it within one page?*

3. Jake delightfully introduces himself to his reader. How does he capture his personality throughout? What is his tone? How does it compare to Melvin's?

> *There are six billion people in the world. What makes <u>me</u> so special? Frankly, I'm not. I've never negotiated a peace treaty. I didn't discover penicillin. I can't make toast without burning it. I've never*

won a Nobel Prize.

In my life, I haven't once successfully refolded a road map. In fact, my most consequential award was a Harlem Globetrotters jersey I won in a 1997 raffle. In seventeen years my most significant contribution to the human race has been my trend-setting use of the word "audacity" in everyday conversation.

Lacking such achievements, it's difficult to project myself as a three-dimensional person on one-dimensional paper. Here, however, is what I <u>can</u> tell you: Though I have the ability to, I have never purposefully hit a nun with my car. I don't like hunting. No matter how many times I vow never to eat Taco Bell again, I always do. I don't have any piercing or tattoos and don't plan on getting either— unless, of course, that satanic cult I've been looking into decides to lower their yearly dues. I swear at my computer. It is not inanimate, so please don't tell me otherwise. When I was eight, I tripped on a basketball and hurt my knee. When I was sixteen, I slipped in the bathroom and cut my chin. I have two scars. In seventh grade little league, I hit two homeruns in one game. I once listened to Bruce Springsteen's "Thunder Road" seventy-four times in one night. I am fluent in pig Latin. I'm not proud of it, but I have been known to wear black and brown in the same outfit. After I saw "The Godfather," I quoted it for weeks, until my friends told me it was annoying. I've often wondered if life just doesn't get any better than a bag of Peanut M&M's and a box of Mike n' Ike's. Recently I discovered that my left eye is dominant over my right, opposite of the norm. Because of this, I like to say that I belong to a minority group. I think bottled water is ridiculous. I drink bottled water. My favorite fruit is the grape, not because of its taste, but because of its aerodynamics.

I'm not a racist, sexist, polygamist, or chemist. I am a conformist, activist, and motorist. I haven't yet found a cure for cancer, but then again neither has anybody else. I've only been allowed to see rated R movies for a few months. My life is just beginning. Grant me a reprieve.

CHAPTER 6

The Antidote for Telling:
Description, Details, and Imagery

If we English teachers ran tattoo parlors, students would have "d-e-t-a-i-l-s" scripted across their foreheads. Details give color, flavor, and voice to writing. While students are working on the various stages of their writing, they need to be reminded often to show their reactions to situations, people, and conflicts. It is too easy to slip into "telling mode," where everything is told and nothing is shown. Vivid description and specific details enhance a personal narrative and recreate a scene. It is one thing to be told that it was exciting to jump from an airplane, it's another to read about "how the wind scoured the scream from my lungs." Since the goal of writing a college essay is to create an interesting account of an event, situation, dilemma, etc., the essay must rise above bland, mediocre writing. Details are the key.

Handout #15 on the CD provides writing samples that illustrate how students descriptively captured a scene that they had experienced. Students are asked to read the passages then discuss how the writers portray their surroundings and how they communicate their reactions in each situation.

▶ HANDOUT #15 ◀

Details Communicate

Read the following student paragraphs. How do the writers portray their surroundings? How do they communicate their reactions in each situation?

1. *Entering the cramped room, I walked over to her bed as she lay there peacefully asleep. In the silence I glanced at the chipped table in the corner where the wilted roses sadly hung from the milk-glass vase. Dried petals dotted the tabletop. Her wedding portrait hung above her head. How time had stripped her of her beauty. She sighed deeply and continued to sleep. Carefully I covered her bare arms with the soft flannel blanket as I bent down to kiss her good-by.*

She struggled to open her eyes yet cracked a faint smile acknowledging my presence, and I was connected to her once more.

2. *The night was thick with the smell of the beer-induced crowd, still perfumed with boxed popcorn and hot dog scents, lingering through the stadium. From my position on the sideline, I could distinctly hear the overly excited shouts from the Dawg Pound and recognize the deep bellows of the air horns echoing off the concave cement stadium. The second quarter clock had diminished and the players rushed off the field.*

3. *Amidst the clamor of hammers and grinding saw blades, a wooden outline gradually rose from the foundation. Over several weekends I pounded in and sometimes pulled out, countless handfuls of nails, helping to lay down the floor, raise the walls, and put the roof supports into place. Gradually the hammered cadence abated, and the house came to life as electrical wiring wove through the walls and ceiling and pipes jutted out of the floor like clusters of periscopes peering out of water.*

4. *Still clenching his lifeless and withered hand, I felt his paper-thin skin loose its warmth. Flashing images of my childhood began to flood my mind once more. Sitting on his lap, sinking into the corner of the corduroy chair, I could hear his voice tickle the back of my neck, and visualize his gray whiskers moving as he enunciated each work of the fairy tale, using different voices for each character.*

5. *I acted like I owned the studio floor by elongating my torso and holding a beautiful <u>arabesque</u>. I would bend down into a <u>ponche</u>, leaping across the studio as if angels had a hold of my limbs and were carrying me, and running so fast and with such ease I didn't think the ride would ever end.*

Word Lists: Working Adjectives and Action Verbs

Whenever I think about word lists, I always remember Robert and his plea for help. A charming and bright student who was determined to shortcut his way to success with quick-fix approaches, he asked one day in class, "Is there a list of adjectives somewhere that we can use to identify the tone of these writers?"

I have always assumed that the best way to improve and expand vocabulary is through reading, so I rolled my eyes at Robert. "A tone list?" I quipped. "Has it come to this? Why not rely on the vocabulary you have learned from reading?" But that was Robert's problem. Later that day he confessed to me that he had sailed through three years of honors English courses and had never *read* any of the assigned novels—instead he listened to them on audiotape.

My admonishment was partly rhetorical: fewer and fewer students today are voracious readers, and unfortunately their vocabularies sometimes reflect that. However, the week after Robert's request for a "tone list," he was vindicated, for I received a copy of *A Guide for Advanced Placement: English Vertical Teams* from the College Board. And there on page 30 was a list of "tone vocabulary." When I showed it to him, Robert beamed.

So—as much as I'd prefer student vocabulary grow from the fertilizer of literature—occasionally I do succumb to the convenience of word lists.

Word lists have their place, but there is a drawback to allowing students to use them in isolation. Students—given a list of fancy-sounding vocabulary—tend to adopt words that do not blend into their style of writing. You are undoubtedly familiar with those thesaurus treasures that leap out at you when reading their essays.

As the SAT approaches each fall, seniors generate a newfound interest in words. To help their cause, I share with them my "Hanging Out with Words" list of SAT caliber vocabulary. In class discussions and in group work students try to earmark those words that have common characteristics (though they may not be synonyms as such) and those that are antonyms. Then the practice sentence-building begins. Eventually they write a descriptive paragraph using several of these words without sounding fake or forced. This process continues intermittently throughout the school year. As an acknowledgement of their ever-growing vocabulary, inevitably I would hear their sweet sarcasm as they shared with me their *copious* notes despite their *gregarious* nature and their *lethargy* at the onset of senioritis.

Handout #16 on the CD provides the College Board's list of tone vocabulary. I found it useful in helping students not only analyze tone in the works they read but also expand and utilize their working vocabulary in their writing. This handout asks students to write a character sketch of a real or imaginary person using some of the vocabulary words on the list.

Handout #17 includes my collection of SAT-type vocabulary words and instructs students to place the subjects of their character sketches in stressful situations which causes them grave concern.

HANDOUT #16

Tone Adjectives

Write a character sketch of a real or imaginary person using some of the vocabulary words on the list below.

angry	boring	joyful	zealous	somber
sad	poignant	peaceful	tired	candid
sentimental	sympathetic	horrific	frivolous	proud
sharp	afraid	allusive	irreverent	giddy
cold	detached	mocking	bitter	pitiful
fanciful	happy	sarcastic	audacious	dramatic
upset	confused	sweet	benevolent	provocative
urgent	apologetic	objective	dreamy	didactic
silly	hollow	nostalgic	shocking	complimentary
joking	childish	vexed	seductive	contemptuous
condescending	humorous	vibrant	restrained	

Source: *A Guide For Advanced Placement: English Vertical Teams*, Copyright © 2002 by College Board. Reproduced with permission. All rights reserved. www.collegeboard.com

HANDOUT #17

Hanging Out with Words

In a paragraph or two place the subject of the character sketch in a stressful situation which causes him/her grave concern using some of the vocabulary words on the list below.

sycophant	sagacious	poltroon	lethargic	prudent
garrulous	gregarious	pusillanimous	ennui	ludicrous
taciturn	lugubrious	munificent	harangue	prodigious
fetid	contumacious	copious	pathos	diminutive
salubrious	obstreperous	plethora	apathy	prostrate
sedulous	pugnacious	paucity	heinous	malevolent
hackneyed	querulous	modicum	tyro	torpid
trite	surreptitious	superfluous	neophyte	
placid	voracious	ubiquitous	fledgling	

Any mention of SAT words elicits memories of Henry, a student who had emigrated from South Korea as a freshman. He insisted on taking Advanced Placement English his senior year because of his quest to enter an Ivy League school and become a politician. To him that meant mastery of multi-syllabic words in order to excel on the SAT. He spent holiday vacations studying word lists and persisted in "dumping" SAT vocabulary into every written exercise. I certainly admired his drive and respected his goals, but I was frustrated because he would not listen to my pleas for clear, concise writing. When confronted with his abundance of awkward sentences, he always became defensive. "But I want to sound like the great authors." I suggested he read Steinbeck.

Then one day, Henry—obviously frazzled and carrying a book of poetry—entered the writing center. "How do you know what the poet meant? How do I know where to begin?" Poetry had become his nemesis. He was desperate enough this time to listen. So we worked together discussing a reading process that helped him paraphrase sections of a poem and verbally share his initial impressions based on the key words and images used in the poem. We talked about vocabulary that could communicate clearly his ideas about the poems. I never missed a chance to discuss the importance of developing a natural style instead of imposing heavy-handed words to impress the reader—which was his mission all along. Then we progressed to "one liners." I bombarded him with a series of daily exercises asking him to state a poet's message in one sentence, the tone in a single word. Eventually he was able to express his thoughts about poems more clearly and succinctly, and this carried over into his narrative writing. Who knows, maybe his fascination with our political system someday will lead him to the halls of Congress. And if it does, he'll be ready to sling the platitudes like a politician—only Henry will sound erudite in the process.

Another source for word lists is *Words That Make a Difference: And How to Use Them in a Masterly Way.* Robert Greenman presents vocabulary in a most unique format. Using "respelling" for pronunciations, he not only defines words but also presents their informative and often delightful applications as used in context by *The New York Times.*

Verb Choices

Students often think of adjectives when they need to expand their vocabulary. I suppose this is a result of the ongoing quest to analyze tone in practically everything they read. But verbs, too, can be powerful tools that can ignite the intensity of a conflict, provide a spontaneous exclamation of joy or dismay, or recreate the serene beauty of a tropical sunset. Though the list on **Handout #18** on the CD is not a sophisticated one, it does offer vivid options for description. On it, students are asked to write a paragraph using several of the words on the list. They can change verb tense or transform them into participles or gerunds.

HANDOUT #18

Concentrating on Verbs

Write a brief paragraph using several of the verbs from the list below. You may change tense or transform them into adverbs, participles (verbs that end with *-ing* or *-ed* and that function as adjectives) or gerunds (*-ing* verbs that function as nouns).

defer	collide	stomp	rant
bicker	shuffle	contrive	flounder
shudder	deviate	relish	decipher
nudge	succumb	capture	pry
pelt	hassle	chatter	slouch
blunder	grouse	rally	converge
malign	swerve	scoff	escalate
thrash	plunge	banish	stroll
avert	alienate	pluck	plunk
ramble	pounce	clinch	glisten

Handouts #19 and #20 on the CD provide exercises for students to rewrite the given sentences to create more descriptive statements. The directions in **#19** require students to reconsider the adjectives and verbs. **#20** directs students to convert the "telling" sentences to ones that "show" by using description and details.

HANDOUT #19

No Bland Sentences Here

Rewrite the sentences below by inserting an adjective before the subject and inserting an adverb somewhere in the sentence.

1. The lady walked across the room.

2. The garbage truck entered our street.

3.   The balloon went up into the air.

4.   My coach was the first to ski down the slope after the snow fall.

5.   The tornado touched down near the farm house.

6.   The dog wanted to go outside.

7.   The mother heard her baby crying.

8.   The car wouldn't start.

9.   The swimmer shivered.

10. Music makes me happy.

HANDOUT #20

Showing v. Telling

Convert the "telling" sentences below to ones that show by elaboration. Feel free to change the structure of the sentences to accommodate your details and descriptions.

1.   The boys skateboarded down their street.

2.   They were lifting weights before school started.

3.   She was babysitting for the two-year-old.

4.   He was trying to fix the muffler on his car.

5.   The boy scouts camped out in the rain.

6.   The contractor was installing a roof on the house.

7.   The mudslide threatened the houses below.

8.   She tried to bake a chocolate cake.

9.   He cut the grass.

10. They searched for the boys.

Photography—Describing through the Lens of a Camera

Just as eyes communicate when a student is ill, angry, or bored, so do they communicate feelings in photographs, sculptures, and portraits. Over the years I have collected photographs and slides of individuals—from sports figures and politicians to children and the elderly—all expressing a range of emotions. Each provides a stimulus for students to describe precisely what they literally see, how they perceive the emotions portrayed, and what their reactions to the photograph are as well. To do so they must engage in selective word choice relying on explicit details and descriptions.

After showing students a variety of photographs or slides, I have them list adjectives that describe the individual and then write a descriptive paragraph placing that individual in the situation that elicits the emotions they describe.

Some helpful sources for this exercise:

America 24/7: 24 Hours. 7 Days. Extraordinary Images of One American Week.

Classic Baseball: The Photographs of Walter Iooss, Jr.

Gladiators: 40 Years of Football Photographs

Look, Think & Write: Using Pictures to Stimulate Thinking and Writing

National Geographic, The Photographs

Paul Strand: Sixty Years of Photographs

Through the Lens, National Geographic Greatest Photographs

Ways of Reading: Words and Images

When They Were Young, a Photographic Retrospective of Childhood

Students know what we mean when we say "show, don't tell." What they may not understand is **how** to change a factual account into one that comes alive. Having them practice this skill will help. After they've had the opportunity to work through the handouts and suggestions I've included in this chapter, I suggest you earmark a few sentences within their essays and ask them to transform them with doses of descriptive adjectives and specific details. By applying these suggestions to their own work, they will begin to comprehend how to convert a lifeless passage into a surrogate experience for the reader.

CHAPTER 7

Revision: Draft after Draft after Draft

Revision can be an open field, and your students easily can get lost among the weeds. Rewriting weak passages can be a tedious task that requires repetitive readings and patience—something not every high school student has in abundance. However, once your students have established a focus and direction for their narrative, you need to convince them that their work is just beginning. Whether it's for their college applications or not, for your students' personal narratives to be successful, you need to prepare them to write draft after draft after draft. It is hard, slowly evolving work. Revisions do not happen overnight—in fact, at some point you should encourage your students to put their drafts aside for a day or two: distance enhances perspective, and a period of mental incubation will help most writers regain an objective approach to the content.

Because some students think their first drafts are perfect, your class may need guidance in identifying problem areas that require rewriting. And as writing teachers we all have experienced students at this stage who are eager to have you dictate what they should write. They want you to tell them exactly how to eliminate what is unclear, awkward or wordy instead of enduring the arduous process of refining their prose themselves. Maybe the most important thing you can teach them is that while they certainly can seek input from teachers, peers, and parents, ultimately any changes in the piece must be their decision.

I participated in a writing workshop that Toby Fulwiler conducted at John Carroll University as part of a state grant that brought together the English departments from three area high schools. Our mission was to collaborate with the university to determine if there was a skills gap between senior-year high school English and freshmen college English. (There was.) During the workshop, Fulwiler discussed the revision process he used with his students in a creative writing class he was teaching at the University of Vermont. As his students worked on their short stories, he would conference with each individually and cite one area that needed attention, such as the omission of dialogue or the further development of a character. But he would point out only one major weakness each week. When the student returned, if improvement was made, he would make another suggestion. And so the semester went with this piecemeal approach (EECAP workshop 1992).

Fulwiler's process encouraged his students because they experienced some level of success with each phase of revision. While few high school English teachers have the luxury of extending the revision process over an entire semester with such singular focus, the process is valid. Highlighting one major problem at a time, such as weak organization or repetitive sentence structure, and having the student work on it exclusively, can insure progress—though it be slow—and provide greater awareness of the essays inherent flaws.

Guidelines for Revision

Students—especially those working on college application essays—seem to courageously pursue the demands inherent in revising because they are fully aware of the stakes involved. As they get started, I encourage them to review their output from every stage of the writing process—their brainstorming and clustering sheets, sectional outline, and each evolving draft. I am a strong advocate of saving drafts, for they document progression and growth. They are the bricks and mortar of thinking.

Handout #21 on the CD provides guidelines for students that have completed their first drafts. It encourages students to revisit what they have written and earmark some of the common errors. Again, tell your students that they cannot address all of these issues at one time. They need to establish priorities with each of their rewrites, for the process extends far beyond mere "editing" where they solely check for errors in grammar and usage, spelling, punctuation, etc.

▶   HANDOUT #21   ◀

Revision Guidelines

- Organization

    If you are addressing a specific question, are you answering all parts of it?

    Do you have a strong beginning? Does the first paragraph grab the reader?

    Are the main sections of the essay in order? Do they follow the sectional plan established during your clustering phase?

Is the essay focused on your purpose and intent?

Does your angle drive the paper? Is it apparent in every paragraph?

Review the first sentence of every paragraph. Does each connect to your angle?

Do the paragraphs evolve sequentially throughout the draft?

Do the paragraphs in the body of the essay provide ample details and descriptions that engage the reader by showing more than telling?

Are there areas that could be eliminated without hampering the strength of the essay? Do you have extraneous information and digressions, areas that are repetitive?

Are there areas that need to be developed more fully?

Are you satisfied with your closing paragraph? Does it capture the impact you want to leave with your reader?

- Style

  Are your ideas expressed clearly and concisely? Can you identify any awkward or wordy sentences or passages? Do you know how to revise them?

  Are action verbs and vivid adjectives used throughout?

  Is your voice maintained throughout?

  Can the syntax be improved? Do subject-verb sentences (**S-V**) dominate and render the writing choppy? Do sentences reflect a variety of grammatical patterns such as introductory clauses, participial phrases?

  Avoid ineffective utterances:

  There is inhibits description. Without it you can tell more.
  >> There is a Monet painting on the wall.
  >> The Monet painting draws the viewer into the soft blues and greens of his garden.

Pretty good straddles. It implies something is OK but not great.

> The party was *pretty good*.
> The party was swinging with the jazz trio.

Nice says nothing.

> I bought a *nice* dress.
> I bought a red satin, strapless dress.

Sort of is indecisive.

> I was feeling *sort of* sad.
> I was sad to learn she was leaving.

Alot = a lot　　How much is *a lot?* Be specific.

Due to the fact that is wordy. One word ("*because*" or "*since*") can replace those five.

Avoid slang and trite expressions: *lucks out, screwed up, out of it, wrong side of the tracks, go nuts, can't handle the situation, dragged over the coals, phat, etc.*

Check your "mechanical" errors—spelling, punctuation, capitalization, etc.

Read your paper aloud. Often your ear can hear the troubled areas more readily than your eye can perceive them.

Less is more. Good writing is a paradox: It eliminates extraneous information, yet amplifies details concisely.

Assessing the First Draft: A "Collective" Conference

I think of the "collective" conference as a "one-on-one": one teacher with one class. It's a time saver for teachers in several ways. It can take the place of an individual conference since teachers can address the entire class with issues apparent in the first drafts that were collected and reviewed. It can provide avenues for correction. It can save time grading since teachers do not have to script repeatedly the common errors on every essay. Transparencies become the vehicle of communication.

After years of teaching writing, I still find that awkward and wordy sentences are the most prevalent weaknesses in student writing. Students may recognize the need to correct them, but most often they don't know how. Writing "wordy," "awkward," or "rewrite" in the margin simply identifies the errors. It does not help the student to execute the needed change. In my frustration I found sharing transparencies that illustrated these and other common errors with students before returning their essays helped the class at large to recognize their problems and implement ways to correct them. A minimalist when it comes to assessing a class set of papers, I use symbols (placed in the margin across from the underlined error) to designate problems, and I write only a brief comment at the end of the paper designating a strength and citing the main point that needs immediate attention. This suffices because I know I will cover much more in class. The transparencies I use are springboards for lively discussions.

I introduce these grading symbols the first week of school and ask students to keep a copy in their notebooks so that I do not have to keep repeating what each means every time a paper is returned.

AWK = awkward, foggy thoughts

W = wordy, runny thoughts

V = vague

? = What do you mean? Clarify

TR = transition

I.S. = incomplete sentence

S-V = subject/verb construction

D = diction

M = modifiers

Sp = spelling (A spelling error is checked only once the first time it is seen.)

Sl = slang, trite

P = punctuation

L = begin new paragraph

AP = apostrophe

Creating Transparencies

Transparencies can be designed to bullet examples of problems while withholding just enough information so we, as teachers, can capture our students' attention with spin-off explanations, questions, and qualifications. While reading a set of essays, I jot down the most recurring errors (which usually pertain to grammar, usage, and those awkward passages) and pull examples directly from the essays. These remain anonymous, never to embarrass anyone. Then after all the class sets are read, I create transparencies. Often, I'll embed humorous quips in these to encourage my students despite having pointed out their drafts' blatant problems. Note that these first drafts are not graded. Doing so would defeat the principles of revision. First drafts are merely first steps, and grading them only encourages students to think of them as finished products.

The transparencies that follow are eclectic examples of how issues can be addressed. They do not provide an all-inclusive list of grammatical rules, nor do they solve all the awkward or wordy expressions. The purpose in creating them is to highlight many of the common errors and weaknesses found in a single set of first drafts while offering solutions for improvement. Besides, by the time students are in high school (let alone writing college application essays), they have been exposed to all the basic rules of grammar and do not need a mega-dose, chapter-by-chapter review.

Every point listed on these transparencies offers an opportunity to provide explanations and class discussions and is followed by exercises that help students practice and reinforce what they have learned. After the main concerns on each transparency are addressed, I share samples of well-written passages and occasionally an entire essay. This facilitates peer sharing since an entire class can read an essay in minutes. And nothing we could say impacts students more than reading a fine essay created by someone sitting nearby. The greatest endorsement young writers can receive is the spontaneous outburst of disbelief from their classmates: "Did someone in this class really write that?" Measuring their performance against those illustrated clearly communicates for them what yet needs to be accomplished.

A word about the time factor. My classes were fifty-five minutes long, so I could present several transparencies with follow-up discussions comfortably within one period. If time ran out, exercises could be assigned as homework. If your class time is considerably shorter, you would have to modify the sequence depending upon the needs of your class.

Sample Transparencies

Transparencies #1, **#2**, **#3** and **#4** on the CD are instructional transparencies that demonstrate some of the principles of grammar and usage. **Handout #22** is a practice exercise of 30 sentences that requires students to correct errors that pertain to the topics previously shown on the transparencies.

Transparency #1 serves two purposes: It illustrates how to achieve variety with sentence formations while punctuating correctly to avoid sentence fragments, run-on sentences, and awkward expressions. **Transparency #2** deals with dangling modifiers, a recurring error for many students.

▶ ## TRANSPARENCY #1 ◀

Common Errors in Punctuation/Sentence Structure

_____ S - V _____ .   simple sentence

_____ S - V _____, and _____ S - V _____ .   compound sentence

When _____ S - V _____, and _____ S - V _____ .   complex sentence

Enjoying _____, the audience _____ .
introductory participle phrase

I wanted to buy a special gift for my friend. Some thing she would like.
sentence fragment

▶ ## TRANSPARENCY #2 ◀

Dangling Modifiers

1. **Tutoring** students after school, **Dad** drove me home.

2. **Correcting** errors on my research paper, the **phone** rang.

3. Having **run** the race in the rain, the **sun** eventually appeared.

4. **Running** into the street, the **car** hit the squirrel.

5. **Searching** for her homework, the **100-pound Lab** crunched it under his paws.

One of the most egregious errors that I hear in the classroom, from the pulpit, throughout the media, and especially in casual conversations is the misuse of the pronoun "I" as the object of the preposition "between." This error illustrates how repeated exposure can render an incorrect construction acceptable to the listener.

Transparency #3 presents practice exercises dealing with subject/object pronouns and the ever-intimidating duo, *who/whom.*

Examples A and B below are difficult constructions. Students readily use *whomever* erroneously in A in response to the preposition "to" which takes the objective case. However, the subordinate clause needs a subject—whoever—making the entire subordinate clause the object of "to."

With sample B the subordinate clause also is object of the preposition "to," but since it has a subject (she), the verb "chooses" in the clause takes "whomever" as its direct object.

A. Give the book to  whoever needs one.

B. I will give the book to 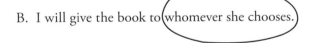 whomever she chooses.

▶   TRANSPARENCY #3   ◀

Subject-Object Pronouns

First Person "I"

John invited Joan and I.

Between you and I, the test was impossible.

Me and my sister are going to the movies.

My brother is younger than me.

Second Person

Your one of my best friends.

Your sister is waiting for you.

Who/whom

subject

1. Who wrote the book? (Whoever, Whomever) wrote it used many interesting facts.

2. Give the book to (whoever, whomever) needs one.

object

3. I will give the book to (whoever, whomever) she chooses.

4. I will drive (whoever, whomever) she wants to the concert.

Transparency #4 deals with apostrophes, possessive pronouns, contractions, and the effect of the passive voice. It also includes a list of "confusing pairs" such as *accept/except, quiet/quite, among/between,* etc.

TRANSPARENCY #4

Apostrophes Show Possession

Adam's ambition		the girls' recital
the officer's badge	singular	the officers' badges	plural
Joan's bracelet		the fathers' jobs
Mr. Jones' car		the Joneses' yard

What's the difference between "Sam and Joe's boat" and "Sam's and Joe's boat"?

theirs
ours
his
hers
whose
its
yours

} No apostrophes with these pronouns

- **Contractions**

  It's is a verb contraction = it is
  don't = do not
  can't = cannot
  wasn't = was not
  haven't = have not
  he'll = he will
  you're = you are
  they're = they are

- **Passive Voice**

  The cake was made by my mother.
  My mother made the cake.

  The sketch was drawn by John.
  John drew the sketch.

  I can't believe the phone call to cancel the tickets was made by my best friend.
  I can't believe my best friend made the phone call to cancel the tickets.

  The hole in the backyard was dug very quickly by my dog.
  My dog dug a hole in the backyard very quickly.

Occasionally the passive voice can be effective:

  The speech was delivered by the president of the club.

Most often, however, the passive voice makes a sentence wordy and inhibits the flow of language.

- **Confusing Pairs**

accept/except	principal/principle
angel/angle	quiet/quite
breathe/breath	than/then
clothes/cloth	raise/rise
compliment/complement	number/amount
conscience/conscious	fewer/less
lie/lay	among/between
precede/proceed	

Follow-up exercises like those in **Handout #22** are distributed after class discussion. If time allows, students can begin correcting the errors in class or complete the exercise for homework.

HANDOUT #22

Revision Practice

Correct the error/errors in the sentences below without rearranging the wording. If the sentence is correct, mark a "C" in the margin.

1. The dog was chasing (its, it's) tail.

2. Because Mars was so close to the earth we could see it in the dark sky.

3. My brother always thinks he is smarter than I.

4. Driving over the speed limit, the car went out of control.

5. Eager to attend the party, her father said she had to stay home to do her homework.

6. Sarah and Sam's lunches consisted of peanut butter and jelly sandwiches.

7. Alice wondered why John always seems so much happier than her.

8. Dad's and Mom's credit cards are used all the time when we go shopping.

9. If the recall is not defeated, (who, whom) do you think will win the election for governor?

10. The after-prom party should be an exciting time with all the raffles and amount of prizes however I think everyone will be tired from all the dancing.

11. Struggling to find a place to park Adam had to circle the lot several times.

12. When he shoots a basket from a distance the crowd roars with delight.

13. (Who, whom) did you buy the gift for last week?

14. Visiting my grandfather in the nursing home I was surprised to learn that he sings along with other residents.

15. My car was tuned by one of the men at the gas station.

16. I wash my car every week to remove all the dirt and tar from the road but I dont enjoy polishing it.

17. We had such a good time at the amusement park and I can't believe how fast the time went.

18. You said your going to the concert on Friday with Dan and his sister.

19. The parade honored the veterans from Korea and Vietnam. A very solemn occasion.

20. My mother has more patience then any of my other relatives.

21. Running a ten-minute mile, the girls stopped to adjust there shoe laces.

22. Donating clothes for my friends garage sale, the sweaters sold quickly.

23. The teacher gave the notebook to (whoever, whomever) needed it.

24. Everyone seems to vacation in Florida over spring break accept me.

25. My piano recital was long but, everyone seemed to enjoy all the performances.

26. I get paid a minimum wage, to mop and sweep all day long.

27. Me and Bill went to the concert together.

28. The students will elect as the class president (whoever, whomever) they think is the best candidate.

29. That painting was painted by one of the seniors in Art IV.

30. When I leave for college I know I will miss many of my friends.

Subject-Verb Contamination

In addition to errors in grammar and usage, a weakness in style that lingers well into the senior year is the repetitive subject/verb sentence. You may be nodding your head in agreement, for I have worked with teachers in conferences and curriculum meetings who unanimously consider this the most perennial problem in student writing. Often students are not aware of this pattern because they are so intent in delivering the content. When they are in the telling mode, simple sentences tend to dominate their syntax.

If students read this passage aloud, they would hear the repetitive, choppy sound of the syntax.

> *In "The Pardoner's Tale" the pardoner is telling the story. A pardoner is a clergyman licensed to collect money for the church. The pardoner is not a good person and sells indulgences to the people. He lies to the people and is one of the primary causes of the Reformation during these times. The pardoner's story is about three men who become extremely greedy and end up killing each other. The pardoner's purpose in telling his story is to teach a lesson in life. He sells indulgences for money in order to make a nice profit for himself. He does not practice what he preaches. This is the key source of irony in this story.*

This choppiness can be avoided by combining sentences, using introductory clauses, participial phrases, appositives, etc., in order to eliminate the tedium of the repetitive structure and provide a smoother flow of ideas. But before students can do this successfully, they need to review the various options available for the transformation.

Handout #23 includes the pardoner passage above and illustrates ways to convert these simple sentences for a more coherent reading.

HANDOUT #23

Sentence Combining

Read this passage discussing the character of the pardoner in Chaucer's *The Pardoner's Tale*. What is your reaction to it?

> In "The Pardoner's Tale" the pardoner is telling the story. A pardoner is a clergyman licensed to collect money for the church. The pardoner is not a good person and sells indulgences to the people. He lies to the people and is one of the primary causes of the Reformation during these times. The pardoner's story is about three men who become extremely greedy and end up killing each other. The pardoner's purpose in telling his story is to teach a lesson in life. He sells indulgences for money in order to make a nice profit for himself. He does not practice what he preaches. This is the key source of irony in this story.

Now analyze the techniques below demonstrating the various ways those subject-verb sentences can be combined for a smoother flow of language.

_____, but _____.   (joining two sentences using *and, but, or,* etc.)

A pardoner is a clergyman licensed to collect money for the church, **but** Chaucer's pardoner is not a good person.

_____, _____.   (using an introductory clause – *since, although, because, when,* etc.)

Since the pardoner sells indulgences, he lies to the people.

_____ing_____, _____.   (using an introductory participial phrase)

Telling a story about greed, he presents himself as a hypocrite.

<u>The pardoner,_____,is not a good man.</u>   (using an appositive)

The pardoner, **a clergyman licensed to collect money for the church,** is not a good man.

A source that offers many examples of sentence combining exercises that can be used in the classroom is *Sentence Combining: A Composing Book,* written by the father of sentence combining, William Strong. For the past thirty years he has published exercises that demonstrate this technique to help students develop a stronger sense of "flow" in their style.

Handout #24 asks students to improve each example by combining sentences and using transitions to improve readability of each passage.

HANDOUT #24

Sentence Combining and Transitions

Read the following paragraphs then revise them to improve the flow and readability of each passage. Consider modifying the sentence structure and using transitions.

1. I was thrilled when my parents said I could have a dog. I love animals. I helped my grandfather take care of his Boxer. We would walk with Barney to the store to buy him dog food, treats, and even a new collar during the hot, summer months. The owner of the shop would give Barney treats. He would give me one, too, usually a piece of candy. I even attended obedience classes for Barney. I helped train him to obey commands. I feel I am well-trained to take care of a new puppy.

2. The storm was getting stronger. The dark clouds moved in. The howling wind began to batter the tree limbs and send leaves swirling to the ground. I could hear the hail hit the windows. It made so much noise. I could hardly hear the weather forecast on the local TV stations. The lightning was severe. It struck a large branch of the towering oak tree. It hit the ground. The house shook.

3. My summer job was not an exciting one. My responsibilities were to clean the tabletops and sweep the floor of a restaurant. I especially hated cleaning up the mess children left behind such as fries, spaghetti, and buttered bread. Their parents didn't notice the mess they created. My job was difficult also because of a strict manager. He would not allow flexible hours. He thought working for him was a privilege. It wasn't. I worked there for two months. I needed the money for college.

4. My first piano recital was embarrassing. My fingers stopped in the middle of the piece. My mind went blank. I panicked. The audience was very silent. I didn't know what to do. Then I thought of an escape. I could run off the stage crying. I looked at my parents. They were smiling. I practiced weeks before the recital. I knew that piece. I stared at the keyboard. I took a deep breath. My fingers began to move. I started over from the beginning. This time I sailed through the piece. The audience applauded loudly. It was a proud moment.

5. I enjoy packing my lunch. Peanut butter and jelly sandwiches are my specialty. The first step is to select the bread. I like whole wheat instead of white. I spread the peanut butter on one slice. It's important to reach all the corners. I spread jelly on the other slice. Raspberry and cherry are my favorites. I am careful not to spread too much on the bread. It will ooze over. The last step is joining the two slices.

6. My mom had a garage sale. She asked me to donate items for the sale. My donations were picture books and old paperbacks. I opened each book. I was lost in childhood memories. Mom would read to me every night. I loved *Bounce and the Bunnies* and the *Frog and Toad* adventures. I didn't donate those. I graduated to paperbacks in elementary school. I did give these to my mom for the sale.

7. I wash my car every weekend. I enjoy spraying it with cold water from the hose. That removes the surface dirt and grime on the tires. I fill a bucket with water and soap. I slop the suds on with a large, spongy mitt. I begin with the windows—front, sides, and back. I rinse the windows. The sides of the car are next. I suds each one separately. It's important to rub hard. The tar is difficult to dislodge. The windows usually remain spotted with water drops. I wipe them dry with a towel. It's crucial not to wash a car in the sun. The rays will cause the water to dry too quickly. This will leave spots.

8. Writing the college essay is a challenging experience. The pressure to write a good one causes anxiety and frustration. Applicants must answer the questions directly. They have to choose a workable topic. Activities out of school often produce interesting essays like summer jobs and volunteering. It's important to decide on an angle or focus for the chosen topic. Telling too much in chronological order can produce a boring essay. Showing what you want the reader to know through descriptions makes the essay more interesting to read. The first draft seldom will be the final draft. Writing is a process. Revising is an

important step in that process that produces many drafts that lead to the final copy.

9. Making pie dough is not an easy task even for the best bakers. The basic ingredients are flour, shortening, and ice water. The important point to remember is that the shortening must be added to the flour first. It must be worked into the flour with a pastry blender or two knives. Then the dough is stirred with a fork to form one large mass. It needs to rest in the refrigerator for about 20 minutes. The last stage is rolling out the dough on a floured surface. It can be difficult to pick up the dough and place it in the pie pan. An easy way to do this is to wrap the rolled dough onto the rolling pin. It can be transferred to the pie pan more easily.

10. I didn't think my father and I would ever speak to each other again after my first driving lesson. He drove me to a street in my neighborhood with a hill. This would have been no problem with an automatic shift. Ours was a stick shift. We started on flat ground. He instructed me to release the clutch while pressing on the gas pedal. I couldn't do it. I kept stalling the car. With each stall his head would bob forward. The tone of his voice told me he was becoming impatient. I couldn't help it. It was a step that was difficult to maneuver. I did manage to move the car forward. We kept going. I was excited. I approached the hill. Any one driving a stick shift car knows how tricky accelerating on a hill can be. I tried. I never made it up the hill.

When the National Writing Project was launched and students began practicing the stages of the writing process, some parents were enraged that grammar and usage errors could be allowed to exist in any draft. English teachers were accused of abandoning the teaching of grammar. What these parents failed to realize is that we teachers had not abandoned the mechanics of writing. We had stopped emphasizing them during the beginning stages of writing, when focusing on grammar can block the free flow of ideas.

Mechanics should be addressed during the revision stages. Banging out ideas and working on expressing them fully and clearly has priority early on. Research has shown that studying grammar apart from writing may produce good grammarians, but it does not necessarily help students become better writers. Writing improves writing.

CHAPTER 8

Revision in Action

Revision skills are acquired through practice. Learning to recognize what is pertinent, what needs to be developed further, and what has to be reduced or eliminated is a difficult journey for most.

Michael, Lenny, and Leila are all basically good writers. They each had strong first drafts: rough, but with an abundance of information to facilitate the writing process. As usual, my approach in working with them was to question their rationale, suggest alternative approaches, and offer verbal support.

As they worked their way through sequential drafts, they each focused on wordy and awkward passages and restructured sections to improve the clarity and flow of their narratives. Receptive to suggestions, each found the journey challenging but never succumbed to mediocrity, for the improvements they made in each draft encouraged them to move on despite moments of frustration and writer's block.

Michael

Michael was asked to discuss his passion for a course he had taken. He was the editor of the school newspaper and he chose an interview format to reveal his love of his journalism classes.

While his first draft was informative and basically error free, it did not represent his style of writing or include his sense of humor. More importantly, Michael recognized that the essay was steeped in telling. After our initial conference, he decided that instead of discussing his entire world of journalism, he would focus on a single task in the development of the newspaper: writing a cutline.

The results illustrate how important an angle can be. His new approach provided Michael with an avenue to share his personality and his writing skills while cataloging some of the techniques he had learned in his journalism class.

Comparing his original opening paragraph with his revised opening demonstrates the effectiveness of "grabbing" readers and "plopping" them *in medias res*. Instead of a clever but sedate introduction, we are thrown into the pressure of the school newspaper's office on deadline day.

[original]

"Solon High School senior Michael Jones announced his passion for studying journalism yesterday, reports say. Jones also announced his plans for studying print journalism well into his college education."

[revised]

"The most important thing in the world right now, the most crucial aspect of life, more important than the elevation of a messiah or the abolishment of all evil, is writing a cutline for this picture. I backtrack in my mind, using what I know about journalism and what I know about writing to aptly describe a photograph of some kid shaking hands with the assistant principal. It's Friday of layout week, and I have 20 minutes to perfect the pages going into this issue of the school newspaper."

His concluding paragraph evolved from an exercise in telling the reader how important his editorship was to showing the satisfaction he experienced when the edition was complete.

[original]

"I know I will come away with more knowledge about journalism, and about life, than I came in with. I will also have so many new friendships. The perk of having an 11-person staff is the closeness of the group. I believe that this responsibility will launch me further into the world of journalism, and it will be a good stepping stone for what I want to do with the rest of my life."

[revised]

"Finally I can distill the page into CMYK coloring and print it out. Rushing to the printer, I meet 10 other people eagerly waiting the arrival of their creations, like a horde of mad scientists. We get our pages and create a Sears Tower of paper. I staple directions for the publisher to a letter from my co-editor, and hand the pile to my advisor. The greatest sense of achievement flows through my veins, as if the nectar of the gods replaced my blood. My advisor gives me an expression of approval as the final bell rings, letting me know that the staff has attained the most coveted award we possibly could: a pizza party on Monday."

Lenny

Lenny was asked to discuss a meaningful experience and show how it had affected him. His first draft clearly reflected his work ethic. His father had provided him with hands-on experience in home repairs. He knew the value of commitment and diligence in getting a job done, even an unpleasant one. His topic, working on the restoration of a dilapidated house, was interesting and certainly illustrated his conscientious efforts at the work site. His voice permeated the draft, and his descriptions vividly portrayed the challenges involved, though his vocabulary occasionally appeared to be forced.

However, especially in the second half of the essay, he had presented several conversations with his best friend, who also worked at the job site. Those digressions—about unrealistic scenarios like what they would do if they won a lottery—were definitely off-topic. I suggested focusing more on one actual task and eliminating all references to his friend. After review, he agreed.

One of Lenny's main stylistic weaknesses was his wordiness. The examples below illustrate how he transformed his wordy sentences by eliminating unnecessary facts and focusing on his word choice.

[original]

Already strapped into my paint-covered working boots, the only preparation I needed for the day ahead was to put on the leather gloves necessary to take the rotten wood out that the team had left from the night before.

[revised]

In my paint-covered work boots and brown, rawhide gloves, I removed the rotten wood from the house that the team had left the night before.

[original]

Tiredly, I yawned while squatting down to reach for the wood, when my best friend yelled down a well-needed, "Good morning." I rushed carrying the meddlesome load to the putrid dumpster in the back of the house, working my way acrobatically through the day's tools and fresh wood which had been strewn ubiquitously.

[revised]

Carrying the cumbersome load to the putrid dumpster in the back of the house, I acrobatically worked my way through the tools and fresh wood which had been strewn ubiquitously.

[original]

By this time I had become confident in my electrical abilities and with each step I became smoother and smoother. However, I experienced a slight rut in this step that caught me off guard. Despite the hour of work, my job proved unsuccessful as there was no electrical current running through the wires.

[revised]

Although I had become confident, I experienced a minor set-back that caught me off guard. Despite the hour of tedious and painstaking work, there was no electrical current running through the circuits.

[original]

Panicking, I decided I must ask for guidance from the owner, but before any words came out of my mouth, I realized that he had already left for his apartment. Identifying the fact that it was just I against the mistake I would have to accomplish this ridiculous burden all by myself. Simultaneous with my thoughts about the painstaking work that lay ahead I become conscious that another factor was thrown in, that I would have to finish before six o'clock because I had committed to play in a league championship baseball game that evening.

[revised]

Panicking, I decided I must ask for guidance from the owner but realized he had already left. Sweat trickled down my forehead when I realized the crunch for time was becoming serious because not only was the boss not here to guide me, but I also had a league championship baseball game that night.

Leila

Leila enjoyed writing. Her first draft revealed this immediately. She had a novel topic, and she communicated it clearly by delightfully capturing her reluctance to endure a strenuous family tradition. Writing it allowed her to realize that the passing of time can transform unpleasant events into treasured memories.

Leila knew how to revise. She would bring to each conference two copies of her essay and take notes as we talked. The improvement she made in the sequential drafts did not involve radical changes, but they were important enough to render her writing more concise and more descriptive. She rewrote the first sentence of the second and third paragraphs in order to create stronger transitions which enhanced the flow of ideas from one paragraph to the next.

[original]

"Growing up in a military family with no roots, my mother and her siblings developed an obsession with establishing a home base."

[revised]

"My mother and her siblings had sucked our family into this tradition because of their obsession with establishing a home base."

[original]

"So way before I was born, the tradition of going to Bob and Norma's for the Fourth of July began."

[revised]

"This tradition usually began with my mother's misty eyes, overcome with nostalgia, as she proudly gazed at the 130-year-old house."

In addition to making the essay more concise, Leila added details that helped to recreate the atmosphere:

"the squeaking of the farmhouse floors"

"the charm of the dilapidated ruins"

"the spider-infested toilet"

The injection of details also improved her account of the children's outdoor exploration.

[original]

"We galloped through the surrounding fields, picked blackberries, and even anticipated the best home display of fireworks I have ever seen."

[revised]

"We galloped through the fields, picked blackberries, and eagerly anticipated the fireworks bursting in shades of red, white and blue."

In the fourth paragraph she included an internal transition that leads to the children's escape from the criticism her mother received.

[original]

"My mom was in her late forties and she still couldn't peel a potato correctly. On the other hand, this farmhouse offered my cousins and I unlimited opportunities to be the imaginative children that we were."

[revised]

"My mom was in her late forties and she still couldn't peel a potato correctly. Eager to avoid cousin Bob's offensive corrections, my cousins and I slipped out the porch door to explore the surprisingly intriguing surroundings."

The revision of the last paragraph demonstrates Leila's awareness that telling the effect of Nora's death was not as effective as showing it.

[original]

"The summer following Norma's death, only a few of us returned; the experience was no longer the same. Sadly, the next year, not a single Taurus station wagon pulled up for the occasion. Reflecting upon this experience, I can say that I have learned the importance in tradition to gluing a family together. Although I have found that the importance of location is secondary to the importance of being together as a family, I now look back, nostalgically, with misty eyes, proud to have such a wonderful farmhouse in our family for over 130 years."

[revised]

"As the years progressed, much to my surprise, I had developed a dependency on this family ritual that had at one time gone unappreciated. Realizing that the importance of this habitual gathering was simply being together with loved ones, I eventually looked forward to this event. Unfortunately, this realization arrived a little late. Norma died shortly after our last visit, unraveling our cherished tradition. The summer following her death, only a few of us returned; the experience was no longer the same. We listened for the nagging instructions, but they never came. A cleaning woman had been hired and a cloud of dust no longer wafted up into the air when plopping onto the couch. The sight of the *National Geographic* collection overflowing the trash can forced all of us to accept this abrupt loss at the farmhouse. Sadly, the next year, not a single Taurus station wagon pulled into the gravel driveway for our annual celebration."

Drafts may not have such elaborate, hand-written corrections as Leila's do. Most students these days are revising on computers. And so they should. Doing so certainly facilitates writing. But there is something special about those scribbled rewrites during the beginning stages that enable a teacher to follow more closely the student's thought process in making changes.

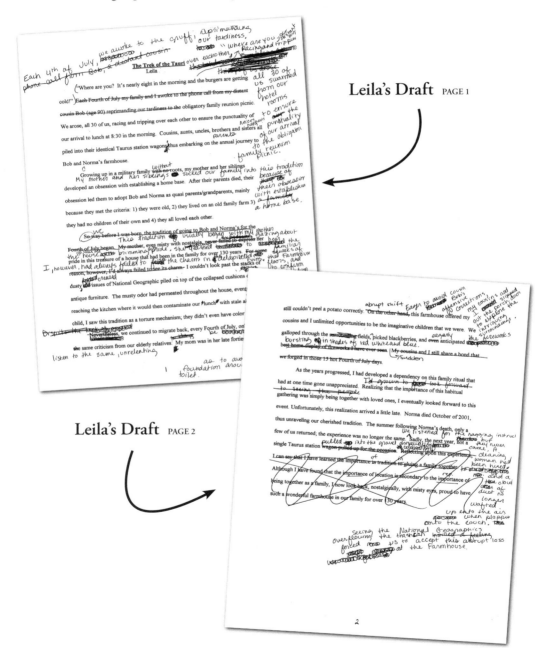

Leila's Draft   PAGE 1

Leila's Draft   PAGE 2

CHAPTER 9

A Selection of College Essays

Students seem to enjoy reading each others' personal narratives. Peer sharing periods allow students to see that their classmates are struggling with the same issues that they are encountering. The opportunity to read each other's work lets them experience the various solutions to the problems of writing. Peer reviews are generally complimentary, particularly in recognizing how powerful voice can be in writing.

The following personal narratives were written to address the "topic of choice" question on college applications. Feel free to share them with your students.

HANDOUT #25

Uyen's Essay

When I was little, I loved to watch my mother bury unripe mangoes. It was always after a bruised and battered day. She would walk to the market with change rattling in her sewn pockets, and a ready voice to haggle with the vendors for the green mangoes lying unwanted by other customers breezing by. She would always win out, and carry them home in her arms. When I watched her, it was like watching a secret rite…her callused, bony fingers scooping white grains into the palm of her hands and gently laying it on top of the green flesh until the mangoes disappeared under the swell of whiteness. Then she would wait, days, weeks, and sometimes months for the mangoes to ripen. When the day came, she would pull them out of the womb spun from grain, peel and slice them up. And we would commence to eat the sweet, juicy, golden flesh content.

One day she brought me a green mango. It was petite lying in her cupped hands. She told me that we were going to bury it, her smile equivocal. I wondered what had happened, but she encouragingly nudged me to the corner of the kitchen were the basin of rice sat. She opened the lid, placed the mango *inside the basin, and scooped a handful of rice into my hands. She told me then, that we were moving to America. I let the rice fall to the ground.*

The only world that I had ever known suddenly slipped between my fingers—the world of hazy afternoons, of scribbled dirt roads with hopscotch boxes, and of loud zooming motorcycles. The grains of rice spilled to the floor, each grain a piece of myself, scattered every which way. My mother frantically tried to gather it up, a frown formed on her brow. She stood tall before me, and simply said, "Life is a miserable journey if we don't bury mangoes."

The night we arrived in America was cold and raining, an instant shock of change from the warmth of Vietnam. I shook as tears streamed down my face; I had never felt so cold in my life. We spent our first night at a cousin's house. I could not sleep, still choked with tears. Then out of the darkness, my mother came to me. She pulled me to the window, her eyes glowing in the moonlight. From her pockets, she extracted a piece of paper. It was a picture of a tall, stately brick building. She smiled unequivocally and said, "This is a very good school. You'll learn many things and can be many things, not like in Vietnam."

Then she placed a mango in my hand. It was ripe. In the darkness, my mother peeled the golden skin and sliced small juicy pieces onto a plate. And we ate in silence, waiting for tomorrow.

Uyen

HANDOUT #26

Amy's Essay

A military gray, big bumpered, jacked-up jeep that reeks of masculinity. One early morning on a throw away day in June, I ran down stairs with the excitement and urgency of an un-potty trained infant. Daddy was to teach me to drive that day, and I couldn't contain myself. I had been loudly awoken with the news that there was a new car outside, but my excitement was quickly tampered when Dad proudly announced it was a stick shift: an obsession of his I had been trying to cure him of for years. "WHAT?" I screamed. "I CAN'T DRIVE STICK. No, don't make me drive STICK!" To whine was useless. When it came to cars, Daddy had the last word. Little did we know the disasters we would encounter.

Stalling in intersections, screeching gear shifts, attacking bumps and avoiding near collisions was the torture that plagued the coming months. Learning to drive stick was like riding the Corkscrew at Cedar point, but practice began to improve my shifting skills. I could finally drive a full day without stalling once. It was an amazing sense of self-accomplishment.

However, just as I thought the worst was over, it started. First with the nagging slow starts in the morning. Then I began to hear the gurgling noises and screeching sound as I shut off the engine. I couldn't take any more. Months of grinding the stick and misuse had taken its toll.

Of course on the day I killed the battery to the point of no return, I had no jumper cables. As I sat on the bumper nervously clicking my flip-flops in the shade of the raised hood, I waited for my dad. He drove up calmly and almost with a smile on his face. His fatherly instincts knew that I had learned the lesson of self-patience. We spent the next three hours surveying the damage, and I received his version of Automobile Maintenance 101. As my mind drifted with the thought of the next week's "jumpstart pop quizzes" and "oil change mind teasers," I changed. I found myself listening to my dad over the bang clang sounds under the hood work. He was different under the hood. It might have been the dim light of the hood lamp or the oil and gasoline smells that clouded my judgment, but he began to make sense. And I had forgotten that despite all his quirky and embarrassing habits, he still knew what he was talking about. From that moment on, and a few hundred dollars later, there was an improvement in the car and in my relationship with my father. I even stopped rolling my eyes at his endless words of wisdom. If I learned anything from this experience, it would be to listen to your father more often and ALWAYS have a pair of jumper cables in your car.

Amy

HANDOUT #27

Kristen's Essay

It was 102 degrees with heavy humidity, and this was only the second day of tennis camp. After hours of grueling drills and circuits, I still managed to run all the way to the natatorium, excited at the prospect of being the first camper in the pool. I raced into the locker room, skating across the newly waxed floor towards the door marked POOL. Bursting open the door, I gasped not only at the gust of steamy, humid air that belted me in the face but at the soccer campers that practically leveled me onto the deck. My dream was shattered. The pool was littered with eighth-grade soccer boys, a lifeguard's nightmare.

I found a tiny spot at the opposite side of the pool, a dark moldy corner where no one was daring enough to venture to. It would have to do. Sweat continued dripping down my back as I walked along the deck. I dove into the water—pure refreshment-- finally, relaxation. All tension was leaving my body. The missed volleys, backhands that went wide, and the out-of-the-court serves no longer bothered me. Nothing could reach me now.

I stayed submerged far under the water feeling safe and secure. Suddenly something brushed against my leg. I opened my eyes and sensed that something was terribly wrong. My body tensed. I saw a body struggling at the bottom of the pool. It was a young boy. His face was turning blue, and he had sunk to the bottom of the pool from the lack of oxygen in his lungs. Terror and panic were evident on his face. I was in shock realizing the seriousness of the situation. We were so far under the water, could I get him up in time?

My instincts immediately took over as I took command of this critical moment. All my training as a lifeguard had prepared me for this emergency. I quickly used the chin lift and put him in a cross-chest control carry, the basic lifesaving maneuver. Thousands of thoughts were racing through my mind while I carried him to the surface. Where were the lifeguards? What if he stopped breathing? Would I still remember how to perform CPR? If only I had known how long he had been down under. His body was so frail. It melted in my arms. Knowing that he depended on me for survival gave me the strength and endurance to reach the surface without panicking.

When we reached safety, I put him down on the deck. He began gasping for air and coughing up the heavily chlorinated water. He would be all right. I was relieved, yet at the same time I was angry. I was furious at the two female guards who were negligent and too busy flirting with the soccer counselors to have watched the pool. My temper flared. "How could you ignore your responsibility! How could you endanger the lives of those who trusted you! What ever happened to all your training that taught you to anticipate danger?" Their silence revealed their humiliation, but that didn't matter. The boy was saved—yet I felt no sense of triumph. My success was flawed by their failure. I felt betrayed.

Kristen

▶   HANDOUT #28   ◀

Adrienne's Essay

My fingers were their own beings by this point. They worked without my direction, pulling and weaving the strands of wiry hair into dozens and dozens of perfect braids, one after the other. Aching and bandaged with sticky white medical tape, they felt as if they had been prematurely stricken with arthritis. My back was becoming sore from standing atop the two-rung ladder, now competing with my fingers to see which could make me suffer more. My hands were well-trained braiding machines. After looking at the thirty identical braids they had manufactured along the ridge of his mane, I was satisfied with my work. The single bare light bulb hanging from the candy-striped tent shed just enough light for me to see that my job had been done successfully. Patting the horse's warm neck, I thanked him for being so patient with my tugging and tying his mane up into the itchy little annoyances that he would soon try his best to rub out.

Only one mane left. Just enough time remained before the sun would come up, the fog would clear, and the trucks would come grumbling into the show grounds carrying grooms and riders to prepare for the busy show day. Darkness and my watch told me the day was just beginning, yet mine had already been in progress for hours. Pangs of jealously taunted my mind. The lucky competitors arrived minutes before they mounted up, never worrying about the grooming, bathing, or braiding of their horses. Having everything handed to them made me envious. However, I learned to be patient. Sighing contentedly, I left the horse's stall with this on my mind—Life could be much worse.

On the way to my next braiding job, the crunch of my dew-saturated sneakers along the gravel road sounded louder than I had ever noticed before. Now I could hear the swish of a pony's tail as he impatiently waited for breakfast. I heard a stallion proclaim his presence with a whinny that was sure to make every mare in the place jealous— so he thought. Every sound had its space here, and seemed to hang in the air just a moment longer.

I couldn't help but think ahead to the time when I could wake up minutes before my class, have grooms tending to my needs, and confidently enter the show ring on my own horse. For now, the behind-the-scenes life would do. It kept me going, knowing that I could experience a side of the horse show that very few ever saw. With these thoughts filling my mind, I almost forgot that I was running out of time to get my final job finished.

Braiding as fast as my throbbing fingers would let me, I started to worry about the grooms arriving before I had finished. The familiar smell of leather would escape from the tack trunks as saddles were pulled out for the day's activity. My final braids would be done just in time. As I snipped off the excess yarn left from tying up the plaited hair, I sighed. Finished. A crackle from the top of the tent broke the placid atmosphere of the morning. The PA system was on, the universal alarm clock for everyone at the show. Once the booming voice greeted the grounds with a hearty good morning, everyone knew that the day of showing was about to get underway. At that point, I became invisible. My work was done and I faded into the chaos. The busy day of shoeing would soon swallow me up, engulfing me in its madness. I left quietly, knowing that without my help, the show would not go on.

Adrienne

HANDOUT #29

Kari's Essay

When I was thirteen, I memorized some Hebrew words and stood in front of my family in a white suit singing to them. I smiled, I kissed a lot of people, and everybody was proud of me. And now I sit in the back of the temple, watching another girl in a white suit, my cousin, during her Bat Mitzvah, and she reminds me of myself at that age: forced smile, hidden confusion. I remember trying to be proud of myself, but I never really understood why. What had I done that was so astonishing? "You're an adult now," they told me. Why? All I did was read something I didn't write in a language I didn't even understand. What maturity, what spirituality does it take to listen to a tape full of gibberish for three months and spit it back in synagogue?

I sit in the back of the temple, not wanting to be there. I have gone dozens of times expecting this to be the time I am finally inspired, but I never get anything out of it. As my mind strays from the prayer book, I notice another girl my age standing in the front row. She prays louder than anyone. She reads straight from the Hebrew, rather than the English-letter transliteration. She bends her knees at all the right times. But a week ago I walked behind her in the hallway at school, listening to her make fun of a fat girl. I have known her to make a habit of sleeping with her friends' boyfriends. Is she more religious than I am?

I sit in the back of the temple as good Jews around me thank God, and I wonder why we have to be there to thank God. If I am standing in a white building wearing a skirt, singing in Hebrew, does that mean more to God than me at home in my pajamas, thanking him in my own words? Is prayer only prayer if it is recited before a qualified rabbi? How can it mean something to God if it doesn't even mean anything to me?

I sit in the back of the temple, thinking about religion. To me it means a system of beliefs. Beliefs don't come from a book, and they don't come from being born into a particular family. It doesn't make sense to me that all the millions of Jews in the world, the millions of separate, different people with different lives, different experiences, different souls could all claim to have the same beliefs. I don't claim to have the right beliefs. I don't even claim to be sure of my beliefs yet. I have a lot to figure out, but I want and deserve the freedom to do that on my own.

I go through the motions of "being Jewish" because it's comforting. Judaism is more a family tradition to me than a religion. From one Rosh Hashanah to the next is a long, unpredictable time. I change, I grow up. But every year I still walk through my Aunt Marci's heavy front door, solid like my family, and enjoy being sucked in. Kisses, smiles, matzo ball soup will always be there. That's what being Jewish means to me. I absolutely, strongly believe in God. I pray. But that has nothing to do with my Judaism.

I continue to sit in the back of the temple, but now I let my mind wander when it wants to. I chant in someone else's words and pray separately, in mine. My religion is my family's, but my beliefs are my own.

Kari

CHAPTER 10

Short-Answer Narratives

Many of the personal narrative questions that your students are going to encounter in their writing lives will require lengthy answers, but some will demand only a paragraph or two. Whether for college applications, tests, or job applications, students need to realize that these short narratives should be crafted in much the same way as full-length essays.

Students are often intimidated by word-count limitations or the minimal space provided on an application. They find it difficult to develop a voice and be creative when they feel constrained.

Reassure them that although their answers to these questions must be short, being forced to be concise isn't a bad thing. They still will use the same skills they have been practicing in their full-length essays: choosing vivid details to frame their voice, sustaining a sequential development of their ideas, etc. Choosing the details on which to frame their voices may be more difficult within the shorter structure, but it is the same skill they've been practicing all along.

Rose—applying to an eastern university—had to respond to a question asking her to discuss an activity she pursued just because she enjoyed it. By focusing on the sound of the piano, she captures the essence of music in her life:

> The piano bench awaits in the thick silence of the shade-drawn room, safely away from the bustle of the street with the zooming of garbage trucks and the frantic scramble for grades, honors and exam scores. I am not a spectacular pianist, and I have never been asked to play at Carnegie Hall. But, nonetheless, I like the sound of the notes pressing into the keyboard as the strings reverberate and imprint the air with the significance of their existence. The notes are an inspiration in themselves that haunt the soul not so much by their melodic themes that capture the emotions, but by the sheer truth of their being. Their ephemeral presence ironically establishes an undeniable permanence into a world where paper records and graying

headstones are the only mementos of past footsteps and smiles. And thus, the piano is an activity that perhaps is not as much a fun activity for weekends as a necessity, an affirmation of living.

Another short answer question asked Rose which department or program of the university appealed to her. Despite her appreciation of music and art, Rose is interested in pursuing a career in biology. In her answer, she delightfully intertwined all her interests:

Renoir whispered to me in ninth grade biology. I was studying photosynthesis and his "Les Grands Boulevards" obstructed my vision. The colors bled into each other, conjoined and overlapped until there were no colors but instead shades, infinite shades that were at the same time dependent and independent of each other. And then the scene faded and I was left in biology and its infinite hues. At that moment physics, chemistry, and biology all melded into the same subject as quantum mechanics contributed to the understanding of the atom, which in turn explained the relationships between atoms in chemistry, explaining relationships in the great biological molecule dubbed chlorophyll. And as physics and chemistry elucidated the excitation of electrons triggering photosynthesis, some of the puzzle of what life is became clear. Thus, to me biology is a great painting of life where the oils of physics and chemistry slip sporadically in and out adding texture and depth to a very complex work. But perhaps the greatest attraction of _____ is the fact that I would be able to see those oils. For although I have attended biology camps and worked with graduate students who have taught me an abundance of knowledge, they were never able to explain the "why" behind a biological function. Heat shock allows transformation in bacteria to occur because it does. At _____ I know that my questions could be answered, and I perhaps could even begin to understand the how and why behind one of the greatest miracles on earth—life.

Adam was asked to explain why he wanted to attend a particular university. In his short answer, he creatively addresses his reasoning by demonstrating how he would be a good match for a school of finance.

From the earliest days of my childhood, I have always been told of my "old soul." At three years old, while other kids were busy watching cartoons, I was questioning the intricacies of human life and behavior. "Do telephone wires act like the brain, sending messages to the different parts of the body?" As I grew, my nature remained. In seventh grade, while the majority still fantasized about becoming professional athletes, I was entirely fascinated and intrigued with the business world. With the help of my uncle, I had already started a stock portfolio from my Bar Mitzvah presents. My admiration continued as I interned for him on the Chicago Board of Trade freshman year. As I learned of technical analyses of the financial markets, I soon became savvy of the head-and-shoulders pattern that was driving the market down on high volume. At Nestle last summer, as the only employee under 20, I established my ability to cope with the responsibilities of a strenuous office environment by working with accounts receivable, accounts payable and placing orders. My strong background in the world of business and management outside the classroom makes me an excellent match for _____.

Modifying Essays to Comply with Length Limits

Occasionally students will want to send their two-page personal statement for one college to another institution as a short response answer. This can be a source of frustration—eliminating portions of a well-written essay while not destroying the impact of the piece. However, besides being useful to the application process, it is very good practice. You may want to consider having your students try this type of condensation as an exercise.

Lindsey experienced this dilemma with two of the main essays she wrote. In her applications she wanted to communicate to each university her pride in her heritage and her passion for dance. Each of the shortened drafts below reflects the arduous process of reducing—without losing—crucial descriptions and passages that reflected her delightful voice.

▶   HANDOUT #30   ◀

Modifying Essays to Comply with Length Limits #1

Original Version

> *Standing in a crowded room, everyone looks the same. My blonde hair, blue eyes and fair skin do not make me stand out, but beneath this everyday appearance is an Italian heart. I have no ties with the Mafia, do not speak as though there are cotton balls in my cheeks, or puff cigars. I do, however, have an appreciation for authentic Italian pasta, family traditions, but more importantly, a great acceptance for all people.*
>
> *Liberata and Lorenzo, my great grandparents, immigrated to the United States with a single suitcase and six children. Unable to read and write they were ridiculed. Changing the family name was their first attempt to appear more American. Like a skinny boy on the sidelines at a football game, who was last to be picked, the family was rejected. They knew their dark hair and olive-colored skin would never disappear. Praying for acceptance in the Land of Opportunity, their struggle was complete. Gripping citizenship papers*

between sweaty fingers, my ancestors promised to pass on an important lesson. Finally, accepted into society, "where all men are created equal," they would pay society back in return. My grandfather, Alberto, was a large man. It wasn't his love for pasta or his genetic make-up, but it was his embracing heart that made him large. While sitting at the kitchen table we often played poker, using a deck of Pittsburgh Pirate playing cards and honey nut Cheerios as poker chips. Peering from behind my cards, I listened to his years of wisdom. Though I didn't completely grasp the concept, I do, however, remember a specific word—acceptance. It wasn't until a family trip to California that I finally understood what my grandfather was quietly saying.

Speechless at the sight of the homeless men and women of San Francisco, I simply wanted to pass by their expressionless eyes. I thought dropping a coin in their half-chewed Styrofoam cup would allow me to feel less guilty about my social status. Hanging in and out of cardboard boxes were their scribbled signs, "Why lie, It's for beer." My short Italian father removed his wallet, only to quickly close it again. Realizing the perfect plan, I helped carry three brown paper bags full of hamburgers. Passing them out, I will never forget the faces and numerous blessings of those complete strangers. These so-called social outcasts were people just like me.

Growing up in the generation of tongue piercing, homosexuality, and religious differences, I will never forget this lesson. Acceptance is a gift. The Italian blood that rushes through my veins is what makes me stand out from the crowd, not physically, but with my compassion.

Shortened Version

Lindsey began by earmarking the details she insisted had to be included—her "Italian heart," the reference to playing poker with her grandfather, and feeding the homeless in California. This—coupled with sentence combining and the elimination of sections she felt could be omitted—constituted the process of her reduction. Here is her end result:

Naturally, my blonde hair, blue eyes, and fair skin do not make me stand out, but beneath this everyday appearance is an Italian heart. I have no ties with the Mafia, do not speak as though there are cotton balls in my cheeks, or puff cigars. I do, however, have an appreciation for authentic Italian pasta, family traditions, but more importantly, a great acceptance for all people.

My great grandparents, Liberata and Lorenzo, immigrated to the United States with a single suitcase and six children. Changing the family name was their first attempt to appear more American. But their dark hair and olive-colored skin were still rejected. Over time, attitudes changed. My ancestors finally gripped citizenship papers from the "Land of Opportunities," and they promised to pass on the legacy of acceptance—a word I will always remember. Playing poker with my grandfather using a deck of Pittsburgh Pirate playing cards and Cheerios as poker chips, I was taught this lesson. It wasn't until a family trip to San Francisco that this lesson became reality.

Walking past the homeless men and women hanging in and out of their cardboard boxes, holding their half-chewed Styrofoam cups and scribbled signs, I realized the perfect plan, distributing McDonald's hamburgers. Their "God Bless You's" made me realize these so-called social outcasts were people just like me. Growing up in the generation of tongue piercing, homosexuality, and single parent families, my Italian blood with the gift of acceptance is my distinction.

HANDOUT #31

Modifying Essays to Comply with Length Limits #2

The following essay captures the essence of Lindsey's commitment to dance. The imagery and the examples she cites communicate her enthusiasm and determination to succeed.

Original Essay

The world goes black, except for the emergency exit at the back of Lincoln Center. Standing motionless in a pose, the only movement is my mind. The seconds it takes the curtains to rise, thousands of thoughts scramble through me. An intelligent man, Henry David Thoreau, once said, "If you have built castles in the air, your work need not be lost; that's where they should be. Now put the foundations under them." Dance has been the foundation in which my life has formed.

Foremost I should reveal that I have a tattoo of a flag on my lower back, to signify the importance of my Italian heritage. I have short nails because I have a bad habit of biting them when I am nervous. I have a skinny scar on my right pinky because I collided with a butter knife due to a desire for a green apple. I have muscular arms and a six-pack stomach. I have a ruby colored birthmark on my stomach and clean lungs because I don't smoke, but more importantly, I have a strong sense of self-discipline. Every time the door alarm sounds entering the dance studio, I am never tired or hungry. In this mindset I complete three pirouettes, jump into an inverted split, and balance in first arabesque in the same time it takes my mom to find her glasses.

Stereotypically, a Saturday morning to a student means waking at noon still in Friday night's attire, only to take a mid-afternoon nap in order to prepare for the next social event. I do not fit this stereotype. For on my side of the spectrum, I am up at six to plaster my hair into a bun. Leaving with my dance bag in one hand and a cup of French Vanilla coffee in the other, I travel the forty-five minute highway commute to the studio. In addition, I have had two adventures over the past summers. My "vacations" consisted of dancing from nine to five, five days a week. Living downtown, I learned to survive solo. Somewhere between budgeting my money and doing laundry or flagging down a cab, I grew up. Self-discipline has brought me into real world situations, which no SAT test could have ever taught me.

I remember pushing myself so hard with so much enthusiasm during a rehearsal that I landed staring toward the ceiling. Despite my balance and coordination, I saw the light. Laughing and optimistic, I peeled myself off the floor. I always try again. Poking at my contact in the mirror, there was sweat dripping in my eyes. My sticky hands started to tingle, like tiny pins when I was trying to sew without a thimble. My left calf trembled when I put weight on it, but I still had stamina to continue. When my teacher asked me why I was still smiling, I quoted Balachine: "First comes the sweat. Then comes the beauty."

I am a firm believer in doing whatever makes one happy, whether it's a nine to five "desk" job, being a full-time mom or a Hard Rock Café waiter. Along with the assiduous dance training comes a feeling that is better than tax deductions, Christmas Eve, and maybe even a first kiss. I am looking forward to living in a cramped New York City apartment surviving on Slim Fast Bars, riding the subway next to the old man who wants me to find Jesus, trying to help tourists find their way to our Lady Liberty, all the while wearing an "I Love New York" T-shirt. I will become a dancer.

When I am performing, anyone could look through to the back of my eyes and see my heart thumping. It is a passion that no one can ever take away from me. It is the same heart put forth when mimicking a favorite singer in front of the mirror with a pair of scissors in one hand as a microphone and no one watching but the dog. I serve my heart and soul to anyone I can capture. This intangible feeling allows me to feel real and then makes dancing feel so right. My seconds of contemplation are over. The curtain has finally finished rising. The music has started. It's my turn.

Shortened Version

Again, Lindsey began the shortening process by choosing the details that she felt had to be retained: the reference to Lincoln Center, her Saturday morning ritual, Balachine's quote, and her dream to be in New York City as a dancer.

The world goes black, except for the emergency exit at the back of Lincoln Center. As I stand motionless in a pose, the curtain rises and thousands of thoughts scramble through my mind. I complete endless pirouettes, jump into a inverted split, and still am able to delicately balance in first arabesque in the same time it takes my mom to find her glasses. I am determined.

On Saturday's I am up at six to plaster my hair into a bun. Leaving with my dance bag in one hand and a cup of French Vanilla coffee in the other, I travel the forty-five minute commute to the studio. I remember once pushing myself so hard, there was sweat dripping in my eyes. My sticky hands started to tingle, like tiny pins when I was trying to sew without a thimble. My left calf trembled when I put weight on it, but some how I had stamina to continue. When my teacher asked me why I was still smiling, I quoted Balachine: "First comes the sweat. Then comes the beauty."

With such assiduous dance training comes a feeling that is better than tax deductions, Christmas Eve, and maybe even a first kiss. It is a breath taking experience that will lead me to a cramped New York City apartment, riding the subway next to the old man who wants me to find Jesus, wearing an "I Love New York" T-shirt. I will become a dancer.

CHAPTER 11

The Quandary of Coaching: A Caveat for Teachers

Coaching students as they work on their writing projects raises a dilemma: How can teachers help students improve their writing without being so invasive that they actually make the corrections for them?

Students learn by doing, and the last thing they need as writers is to lose control of their writing. While making corrections outright is certainly quicker and less frustrating than teaching students to recognize areas that need attention, it does not help them directly. Not only will they not learn as much, correcting their errors also compromises the validity of their writing.

Before joining my school's guidance program as a writing consultant, I tended to control each conference, readily sharing my perception of the student's problems and offering immediate remedies. Now—after working with hundreds of seniors during the first three months of school—I take a more hands-off approach. I rely on a questioning strategy that guides students to discover the troubled areas for themselves. The guidelines below illustrate the approach I use.

Teacher Guidelines for Conference Coaching

- Do not accept a paper that is tossed at you without dialogue. A teacher's position is to provide input, not to proofread and revise the paper. Students must assume control as authors even though they may be reluctant to do so.

- Discuss the narrative before making suggestions for corrections. Ask the student to elaborate on the essay's main purpose and to discuss the strengths and weaknesses as the student perceives them. This should reveal why the student is seeking help. Use questioning techniques that elicit more than a simple "yes" or "no" response.

- Find something positive about the writing that you can share with the student.

Discuss what you do not understand. Sometimes determining cause and effect helps to clarify.

- Help students to identify problem areas. Asking them to read sections of the paper aloud often helps them recognize the awkward or wordy passages and repetitive syntactical patterns (such as subject-verb sentences) that make writing feel choppy to the reader.

- Highlight patterns of mechanical errors instead of citing each instance. Refer the student to texts that provide models of good writing and that refresh their knowledge of grammar. But encourage them to avoid the thesaurus. Too often students are eager to impress and resort to using uncomfortable vocabulary that is out of sync with their style. This is especially true with inflated adjectives.

- Try coaching without pencil or pen in hand. At most, simply mark the troubled areas and have the student script in the margin ways to improve the passage. Every English teacher on the planet has a compulsion to mark and correct. That's our nature. But running a dialogue with students—and having them make their own notes in the margins of their papers—encourages them to think of their own approaches to correcting weak writing. Having students bring two copies of the draft facilitates this dialogue.

- Be careful that students do not become so dependent on your input that it stifles their ability to critically revise.

All of us who have helped students with their writing know that pointing out problem areas can insult or alienate a young author. Sharing a piece of writing at any age is like exposing your soul. You become vulnerable. Having someone designate the flaws can be painful and frustrating.

One approach that helps to assuage students' anxiety during review is tempering the image of you as the all-knowing teacher. When students say they're leery of writing to you from college because you'll probably mark all the errors on their letters, they're reacting to the red-pen attitude that most people associate with English teachers. Try to cultivate an attitude of "writer talking to writer" in your conferences. Assure your students that the suggestions you make are just that—suggestions. They do not have to be implemented. The multiple decisions made during revision—eliminating, elaborating, correcting—must be determined solely by the student.

Coaching v. Authenticity

Colleges, too, are concerned about the extent of coaching involved with college-application essays. Although some coaching is expected, many are beginning to address the issue of compromised authenticity.

Like teachers who combat the plague of plagiarism by turning to websites such as www.turnitin.com some colleges and universities may require applicants to submit a graded writing sample from their English classes to compare with their personal essays. Many universities also include a statement for students to sign, certifying that all information and essays are authentically theirs. For example, the Common Application includes the following: "I certify that all information in my application, including my Personal Statement, is my own work, factually true, and honestly presented."

In reality you undoubtedly will not conduct individual writing conferences with each of your students. But when you do have the occasion to conference, hopefully the guidelines highlighted in this chapter will provide you with a workable approach that helps your students while encouraging them to take charge of their own writing.   §

CHAPTER 12

Writing the College Recommendation

An important factor in the college application process is the teacher recommendation. In a single letter you can sum up many facets of your students' personalities and their potential for success more concisely than all the statistics included in their applications. Your recommendation *can* make a difference.

Staff members, especially those not involved in the language arts, often ask for suggestions that will help them write a stronger endorsement of their students. The following guidelines, based on the tenets of good writing discussed in the previous chapters, should help teachers in all disciplines write a meaningful recommendation.

Considering all your daily obligations, writing these recommendations can be a burdensome task. And some of you, such as the junior English teacher, face an onslaught of requests each fall. When a student asks you for a recommendation, do not hesitate to tell your students how long it will take to produce the letter that they are requesting. Hopefully, seniors have been indoctrinated to expect a waiting period of several weeks—and to submit a thank-you note afterwards.

Before beginning to write recommendations for students, have them submit to you a list of their activities and interests—especially those they pursue apart from school, such as their jobs, hobbies, volunteering experiences, etc. This will provide a more comprehensive view of the child who sits before you in class each day.

Brainstorming the Content

- Consider how you perceive the student. What one word captures the essence of the student's personality?

- How is the student's academic performance?

- What character trait or accomplishment will you remember long after the student is gone?

- What is the student's greatest strength?

- Have you worked with the student in a club or activity outside of class?

- Is the student

  o creative? articulate in expressing ideas, and feelings?
  o perceptive when dealing with complex issues?
  o flexible in adapting to change?
  o humble? unassuming?
  o upbeat and cheerful?
  o pensive? unassuming?
  o sensitive and kind?
  o goal oriented?
  o a problem solver?
  o a team player? an enthusiastic leader?

- Does the student

  o display self-control in trying situations?
  o take risks with valid rationale?
  o have a disciplined work ethic?
  o accept criticism? assume responsibility?
  o have a sense of humor?
  o command respect from peers? from staff?
  o reveal an awareness of current affairs?
  o get involved with community issues?

- If you have sponsored an activity involving the applicant, be sure to include that information.

Organizing

- Develop a basic organizational plan by grouping your brainstorming by related subjects. For example, circle items pertaining to scholarship, then to attitude, to potential, etc. Those circles will represent the basic sections of your recommendation. Then determine the order of the topics you plan to discuss.

  Some people can perform this prewriting process mentally, but for most, working with a list helps. (Naturally, you should forget about sentences, spelling, and grammar at this stage.)

- Pick the driving focus of your recommendation, the main impression of the student that you will develop in each paragraph to prevent it from being a collection of unrelated facts.

- What will be the opening statement that will draw your reader into the recommendation? Often quoting from one of the student's essays is effective.

- Introduce yourself and your relationship to the student somewhere in the first paragraph.

- Consider those transitional links that provide a smoother flow such as *in addition to, however, although,* etc. as you move from paragraph to paragraph.

- Think about your conclusion—Your closing words will leave the reader with a strong indication of your endorsement. Note the difference:

> I recommend Suzie Cue for admission. She will do well in college.

> I heartily recommend Suzie Cue for admission to _____ University. She is one of the most talented and conscientious students I have taught. Because of her enthusiasm to search and discover and her determination to succeed, she will make many meaningful contributions to the university. This is a young woman with a most promising future.

Style and Voice

As important as voice is in a student's personal narrative, so is voice crucial to your recommendation. How will you capture the spirit of that enthusiastic student, the passion of the scholar, the charm of the class president?

A yearly quandary: what to do when a student who does not excel in your class or in any extracurricular activities asks you to write a recommendation. Writing a stellar endorsement for an outstanding student is easier than creating a recommendation for the less-accomplished "nice kid" who does not shine in class. But no one wants to write a lackluster recommendation. If you work to let the specific examples speak for you, your dilemma can be resolved more easily. For example, Johnny may not be a stellar student, but you can relate that he always manages to turn in his assignments on time despite working thirty hours a week.

And remember, often what you choose *not* to say can communicate what you really mean *to* say.

- **Examples and details**

  One of the most important elements in developing your writing voice is providing specific examples and details. This will rescue you from creating a generic stamp of approval. What distinguishes this student from others? It's not enough to say the student is "conscientious." Explain why. Show how.

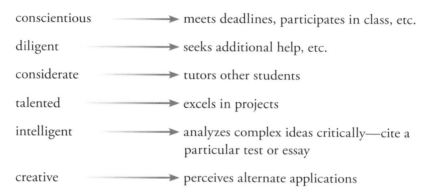

conscientious	meets deadlines, participates in class, etc.
diligent	seeks additional help, etc.
considerate	tutors other students
talented	excels in projects
intelligent	analyzes complex ideas critically—cite a particular test or essay
creative	perceives alternate applications

- **Diction**

  Also important is your word choice, particularly your use of vivid adjectives. For example, does the student have a delightful personality and a demeanor that others find endearing? Is the student sensitive to the needs of others?

  Avoid banal words such as *nice* or *normal*, and trite expressions such as *happy as a lark, bundle of energy, ball of fire*, etc.

  Whatever your "natural" vocabulary, feel comfortable using it and try to be precise in expressing your ideas clearly.

Final Considerations

- **Audience**

  When writing, always consider your audience. What would be your reaction to your recommendation if you were the admissions officer reading it? Are you satisfied with the overview you are presenting?

- **Revision Checklist**

  o   Check the basic organization for a logical content flow.

  o   Are your transitions effective? Does each paragraph lead smoothly into the next?

  o   Rewrite those awkward and wordy areas.

  o   Do you have adequate details and descriptions?

  o   Have you checked for spelling and grammar errors?

- **Length**

  Remember, good writing is a paradox. It provides ample details yet is concise. Much can be said in about a page or so.

  Although college applications often provide space for you to write your recommendation, I strongly suggest composing your letter on your computer (single spaced with block format), printing it on school stationery, and attaching it to the back of the form. (Don't forget to include the date.) Admissions officers are sometimes reading several recommendations for every application. Reading handwritten comments slows the process considerably.

SAMPLE RECOMMENDATION

Date _____

To Whom It May Concern:

Whimsical and enthusiastic, Maggie charmed her classmates each day with her upbeat episodes of teenage angst. Her cork-screw, auburn hair seemed to bounce in synchronization with her emphatic tone. As she spoke, everyone listened. This ability to relate to others is one of Maggie's strengths. Her people skills are outstanding. Kind and sensitive, she endears herself to others. This is evident in the many leadership roles she has assumed with Key Club, National Honors Society, volleyball, and her volunteer work at a nursing home.

In addition, she is conscientious and diligent in regard to her studies. She meets every deadline and pursues each assignment thoroughly. Her comprehension of literature was apparent in the analytical essays she wrote discussing Hamlet's turmoil, Macbeth's ambition, Milkman's search for his roots in *Song of Solomon,* and Swift's use of persona in *Gulliver's Travels.* The insight she brought to poetry and nonfiction selections often helped others in the class to comprehend better the inferential meanings. Maggie asked intelligent questions and displayed a desire to learn. When confronted with challenging questions, she demonstrated her ability to probe and analyze.

Beyond analyzing literature, Maggie is a talented writer and poet as well. She can capture her feelings in vivid imagery and has a voice in her writing that engages her reader. Her writing continued to improve throughout the year because she was receptive to suggestions and never balked at the tedium of revising draft after draft. I included one of her narrative essays as an example of good descriptive writing in a writing workshop for high school English teachers this year. One of her poems was published last year in the school's literary magazine and won second place in the county library writing contest. Her work on the school newspaper also reflects her writing skills. Her commentaries in her monthly columns are interesting to read and have generated comments from the student body at large.

Maggie is a lovely young woman with a most promising future. I heartily recommend her for admission to _____, for this is a student who will take advantage of the opportunities offered and make meaningful contributions to campus life. Her work ethic and people skills will continue to guarantee success for this talented senior. It truly has been my pleasure to have worked with Maggie.

Sincerely,

(**4 spaces**)

Mary Jane Reed

WORKS CITED

Blau, Sheridan. <u>The Literature Workshop: Teaching Texts and Their Readers</u>. Portsmouth: Heinemann, 2003.

Fulwiler, Toby. Early English Composition Assessment Program Workshop. John Carroll University, University Heights, OH, 1992.

Greenman, Robert. <u>Words That Make a Difference: And How to Use Them in a Masterly Way</u>. Delray Beach: Levenger Press, 2003.

<u>A Guide For Advanced Placement: English Vertical Teams</u>. New York: College Board, 2002.

Heiser, Beth. Telephone Interview. 8 October 03.

Kingsolver, Barbara. <u>Small Wonder</u>. New York: Harper, 2002.

Lamott, Anne. <u>Bird by Bird</u>. New York: Anchor Books, Doubleday, 1994.

O'Conner, Patricia T. <u>Woe Is I</u>. New York: Putnam Books, 1996.

Paul, Bill. <u>Getting In: Inside the College Admissions Process</u>. Cambridge: Perseus Publishing, 1995.

Schamberger, Scott. Telephone Interview. 19 September 2003.

Strong, William. <u>Sentence Combining: A Composing Book</u>. 3rd ed. New York: McGraw-Hill, 1994.

Supple, Phyllis. Telephone Interview. 18 September 2003.

Truss, Lynne. <u>Eats, Shoots & Leaves: The Zero Tolerance Approach to Punctuation</u>. New York: Gotham Books, 2004

Wagner, Kay. Telephone Interview. 24 September 2003.

Wilbur, Richard. "Richard Wilbur on Robert Frost." <u>Poetry Speaks</u>. Ed. Elise Paschen and Rebekah Presson Mosby. Naperville: Sourcebooks, 2001.

Willard, Nancy. "Nancy Willard on Denise Levertov." <u>Poetry Speaks</u>. Ed. Elise Paschen and Rebekah Presson Mosby. Naperville: Sourcebooks, 2001.

Zinsser, William. <u>On Writing Well: The Classic Guide to Writing Nonfiction</u>. 6th ed. New York: HarperResource, 2001.

NOTES

NOTES

NOTES

NOTES

NOTES

CD CONTENTS

Handout_01: Writing Personal Narratives

Handout_02: Beginning the Personal Narrative

Handout_03: Brainstorming

Handout_04: Prewriting Practice

Handout_05: Clustering

Handout_06: Sample Clustering

Handout_07: Discovering the Angle

Handout_08: Opening Paragraphs

Handout_09: Comments on the Opening Paragraphs

Handout_10: Revised Opening Paragraphs

Handout_11: The Function of Transitions

Handout_12: Transitions as Links

Handout_13: Tuning in to Voice

Handout_14: Voice in Student Narratives

Handout_15: Details Communicate

Handout_16: Tone Adjectives

Handout_17: Hanging Out with Words

Handout_18: Concentrating on Verbs

Handout_19: No Bland Sentences Here

Handout_20: Showing v. Telling

Handout_21: Revision Guidelines

Handout_22: Revision Practice

Handout_23: Sentence Combining

Handout_24: Sentence Combining and Transitions

Handout_25: Uyen's Essay

Handout_26: Amy's Essay

Handout_27: Kristen's Essay

Handout_28: Adrienne's Essay

Handout_29: Kari's Essay

Handout_30: Modifying Essays to Comply with Length Limits_1

Handout_31: Modifying Essays to Comply with Length Limits_2

Transparency_01: Common Errors in Punctuation/Sentence Structure

Transparency_02: Dangling Modifiers

Transparency_03: Subject-Object Pronouns

Transparency_04: Apostrophes Show Possession

> NOTE:
> In order to open these files on your computer, you will need to install the included Adobe Acrobat Reader™ application.